Land-Water Management and Sustainability in Bangladesh

Indigenous sustainability and environmental management cannot be understood apart from a community, its traditions, and ways of practices. Interest in Indigenous environmental sustainability has grown steadily in past years, reflecting traditional cultural perspectives about the environment and developing research priorities.

This book explores the ways one Indigenous community, in the Chittagong Hill Tracts in Bangladesh, has reinvented the meaning of sustainability using traditional knowledge to blend traditional sentiment with large-scale dislocations within their own communities and international economy. This book includes up-to-date research on meanings and implications of Bangladeshi Indigenous sustainability, which focuses on relationality, traditional knowledge, spirituality, and hybridity. Environmental protection and Indigenous land-water rights have been ignored in the region, and minimal research exists on these intersecting issues, both locally or internationally. *Land-Water Management and Sustainability in Bangladesh* addresses this gap in an examination of postcolonial Indigenous communities' complex and shifting relationships to nature and in relation to discrimination and oppression regarding Indigenous land and rights. The book contributes to both the research literature and on-the-ground practice in inspiring a new culture of sustainability in Indigenous regions.

Bringing together community engagement, activism, critical research, and scholarship to advocate for socioenvironmental justice and trans-systematic sustainability of cross-cultural knowledge, the book will be of interest to academics in a variety of disciplines, including environmental policy, conservation practices, Indigenous studies environmental sustainability, anthropology, American studies, Asian studies, and ethnic studies.

Ranjan Datta is an SSHRC Banting Postdoctoral Fellow in the Johnson Shoyama Graduate School of Public Policy at University of Regina, Canada. His publications include *Responsibilities for Land and Reconciliation* and *Reconciliation in Practice: A Cross-cultural Perspective* (both forthcoming).

Routledge Contemporary South Asia Series

The Rule of Law in Developing Countries
The Case of Bangladesh
Chowdhury Ishrak Ahmed Siddiky

New Perspectives on India and Turkey
Connections and Debates
Edited by Smita Tewari Jassal and Halil Turan

The Judicialization of Politics in Pakistan
A Comparative Study of Judicial Restraint and Its Development in India, the US and Pakistan
Waris Husain

Employment, Poverty and Rights in India
Dayabati Roy

Bangladesh's Maritime Policy
Entwining Challenges
Abdul Kalam

Health Communication and Sexual Health in India
Interpreting HIV and AIDS Messages
Ravindra Kumar Vemula

Contemporary Literature from Northeast India
Deathworlds, Terror and Survival
Amit R. Baishya

Land-Water Management and Sustainability in Bangladesh
Indigenous Practices in the Chittagong Hill Tracts
Ranjan Datta

For the full list of titles in the series please visit: www.routledge.com/Routledge-Contemporary-South-Asia-Series/book-series/RCSA

Land-Water Management and Sustainability in Bangladesh

Indigenous Practices in the Chittagong Hill Tracts

Ranjan Datta

LONDON AND NEW YORK

First published 2019
by Routledge
2 Park Square, Milton Park, Abingdon, Oxon OX14 4RN

and by Routledge
52 Vanderbilt Avenue, New York, NY 10017

First issued in paperback 2020

Routledge is an imprint of the Taylor & Francis Group, an informa business

© 2019 Ranjan Datta

The right of Ranjan Datta to be identified as author of this work has been asserted by him in accordance with sections 77 and 78 of the Copyright, Designs and Patents Act 1988.

All rights reserved. No part of this book may be reprinted or reproduced or utilised in any form or by any electronic, mechanical, or other means, now known or hereafter invented, including photocopying and recording, or in any information storage or retrieval system, without permission in writing from the publishers.

Trademark notice: Product or corporate names may be trademarks or registered trademarks, and are used only for identification and explanation without intent to infringe.

British Library Cataloguing-in-Publication Data
A catalogue record for this book is available from the British Library

Library of Congress Cataloging-in-Publication Data
A catalog record for this book has been requested

ISBN 13: 978-0-36-758482-5 (pbk)
ISBN 13: 978-1-138-35274-2 (hbk)

Typeset in Times
by Apex CoVantage, LLC

Printed in the United Kingdom
by Henry Ling Limited

Dedicated to my mom (Amyo Datta) and the Laitu Khyeng Indigenous community whose love, support, and generosity allowed me to pursue every dream I ever had with the full confidence that I could achieve anything that I set my mind to.

Contents

List of figures and tables viii
Preface and acknowledgments ix

1 Introduction 1

2 Relational theoretical framework and implications for land, management, and sustainability 22

3 Participatory action research and researcher responsibilities 35

4 Traditional meanings of land-water 55

5 The community's perceptions of meanings of management 64

6 The community's perceptions of current management 84

7 The community's perceptions of environmental sustainability 104

8 Youth responsibilities for sustainability 116

9 A call to implications: guiding principles for environmental sustainability 125

10 Concluding remarks 133

References 135
Index 146

Figures and tables

1.1	CHT map	15
4.1	Land, water, and spirituality spirits	56
4.2	Water spirituality	57
4.3	Water knowledge	60
5.1	The agriculture domain	65
6.1	Profitable plantation project over natural forest	91
8.1	Traditional Jhum and plain-land cultivation	118
8.2	Traditional clothes-making	121

Tables

3.1	Pattern and subpattern coding	47
5.1	Traditional administrative structure, land, and water management	71

Preface and acknowledgments

This book was a ceremonial journey for me. As I reflect on my ceremonies as a researcher, I am reminded that being a minority researcher working with Indigenous people and communities involves a journey of learning that can be both empowering and rewarding. Along this journey, it is vitally important that I form authentic relationships with the people I work with. I am not worried about challenges to my research training and ways of being. I remind myself that there will be times in the research relationship when I am the researcher who is seeking objectivity but also times when I am looking to build relationships. My ceremonies taught me that as a researcher both becoming and sharing are reciprocal.

In my research ceremonies, I learned that research is relational responsibility. As community-based researchers we should not look for "[r]ight or wrong; validity; statistically significant; worthy or unworthy: value judgements lose their meaning" (Wilson, 2008). Through this research, I suggest that we need to find out "[w]hat is more important and meaningful is fulfilling a role and obligations in the research relationship – that is, being accountable to your relations" (Wilson, 2008, p. 77). With the guidance of my ceremonial research journey, I learned that as a researcher my empathy, relationships, and participants are a worthwhile part of my research life. Research must be a relationship-building process for self-determination and social justice; otherwise, it should not be conducted.

My research has shown that research has always been part of our everyday lives, and we must reclaim it and own it. In ceremony, research is a process. It is grounded in emotional and cognitive resonance. This process has the potential to increase understanding of the interconnectivity between researcher and participants across sociocultural differences and "motivate them to work toward cross-cultural coalition building" (Chang, 2008, p. 52). I learned from this process that a relational research framework could enable researchers to explore self in the presence of others to gain a collective understanding of their shared experiences. Critical probing of one another is a vital step in the collaborative process (Datta et al., 2015; Wilson, 2008).

Ceremonial research is both a method and a paradigm of decolonization (Datta et al., 2015). I assert that research should be identified, initiated, formulated, led, conducted, interpreted, presented, and owned by the participants in the community because they are the ones most impacted by particular social issues. Research is for me an everyday practice or ceremony that consists of translating, advocating, and building reciprocal relationships; it is not only *data collection*.

In listening to the stories of Indigenous Elders and Knowledge-holders. I have been reminded of how storytelling can positively contribute to Indigenous ways of understanding environmental sustainability. I have seen how stories have an ability to provide comfort, to heal. They are also cyclical, continuous, and never-ending because as one draws to a close, another is beginning. I learned that Indigenous stories are based on respect, reciprocity, and thoughtful action.

Ceremonial research is swinging back to a more conventional scientific inquiry in reaction to the ever-increasing production of self-introspection that lacks methodological transparency. As a relational researcher I have learned that decolonization is not a checklist because knowledge is relational; it must be constantly communicated, negotiated, and agreed upon with honest and sincere hearts. Like Kovach (2010), I believe in "decolonizing one's mind and heart . . . by exploring one's own belief and values about knowledge and how it shapes practices. It is about examining whiteness. It is about examining power. It's ongoing" (p. 169). It does not involve the infamous Institutional Review Board, nor does it embrace any predetermined yet abstract research ethics. Instead, it must uphold relational accountability (Wilson, 2008). I believe that research is, and must be, a relationship-building process. If anyone involved in the process is not interested in cultivating solidarity for self-determination and social justice, the research should not be conducted. This is similar to Wilson's (2008) work that research is relational, I also echo that research must be democratized and deprofessionalized so that the expertise, skills, resources, practices, and products of research are in the hands of the people at the margins. Research (producing knowledge) and pedagogy (transferring knowledge) must be integrated as the core of the grassroots movement because knowledge is power (Foucault, 1979) and liberation must be rooted in praxis (Freire, 2000).

My ceremonial journeys throughout this book taught me how to take a political stand for participants, how to be critical in learning, how to be part of participants' land-water struggle, and how to create a scholarship to advocate for systematic change and trans-systematic environmental sustainability of *diverse* knowledge (in both science and social science). However, we also need to be careful to ensure structure and guidelines accommodate the fundamental concept of *diversity*, because "no single Indigenous experience dominates other perspectives, no one heritage informs it, and no two heritage produce the same knowledge" (Battiste, 2013, p. 66). In creating institutional and systematic change, we need to deeply follow the United Nation Declaration of the Rights of Indigenous People and a relational responsible space. A relational responsible space is a theoretical and action-based space for both humans and nonhumans. It is a space for retreat, reflection, and dialogue to share understanding and to work together to create *a shared future*. Within this relational space it our responsibility as a researcher to ensure that our research is benefitting participants' community.

For this research opportunity first, I would like to thank the Laitu Khyeng Indigenous Elders, Knowledge-holders, leaders, and youths participants who so warmly welcomed me to the community and provided opportunities to learn their land-water management and sustainability stories. I am also enormously grateful to my four coresearcher participants from Laitu Khyeng Indigenous community – Nyojy U. Khyang, Hla Kray Prue Khyang, Hla Aung Prue Kheyang, and Mathui Ching Khyang – for joining in this research team and for your continuous support.

I want also to thank Dr. Marcia McKenzie for being motivating, encouraging, and enlightening mentor to me for this research. I appreciate all her contributions of time, ideas, and inspiration to make this research experience productive and stimulating. I am also grateful to Drs. Alex Wilson, David Natcher, Maureen Reed, and Manuhuia Barcham for your encouragement and untiring constructive criticism. I also thank my friends (too many to list here but you know who you are!) for providing needed support and friendship.

I am extremely grateful for the financial contributions provided to me by the International Development Research Centre (IDRC) though the Dr. Rui Feng Doctoral Research Award, which enabled me travel to Bangladesh and work with the Laitu Khyeng Indigenous community and collect data. Special thanks also to the College of Postdoctoral and Graduate Studies and Research (PCGSR) and the School of Environment and Sustainability funding, which supported my research journey.

Last but not least, I owe a lot to my mom, who encouraged and helped me at every stage of my personal and academic life and longed to see this achievement come true. I deeply miss my mother Amyo Datta, who is not with me to share this joy, but her spirit is always with me. I love you, Ma!! I am thankful to my wife, Jebunnessa Chapola, for your love, dreams, support, and sacrifices. Without your support and encouragement, I would not have made it. Thank you my sweet daughters: Prarthona and Prokriti, for your love and inspiration.

1 Introduction

Interest in Indigenous environmental sustainability has grown steadily in past years, reflecting traditional cultural perspectives about the environment and developing research priorities. This book is a vehicle for publishing up-to-date research on meanings and implications of Indigenous sustainability, which focuses on relationality, traditional knowledge, spirituality, and hybridity. Relevant areas include land, water, traditional management, sustainability goals and expectations, scientific and state development projects, and environmental problems. Although the underlying ethos of this research is focused on an interdisciplinary approach, the theoretical framework is relational.

An increasing number of educators, social and environmental activists, researchers, and resource managers are eager to find ways to support – effectively, ethically, and appropriately – inclusion of Indigenous knowledge (IK) into environmental resource management initiatives. Yet IK is not simply local ecological knowledge with a cultural twist. IK comes from both the physical and spiritual realms (Berkes, 2008; Cajete, 2000; Castellano, 2002) and involves intimate land-water relations with the natural world, drawing on a set of perspectives and paradigms that may provide significant benefits to non-Indigenous resource managers trained in Western scientific methods. This book addresses these epistemological, and ultimately, cosmological differences: *Examine how to bring traditional Indigenous land-water customs and practices into environmental resource management policies and education that recognize social and environmental relations for more sustainable ways of being in interdisciplinary communities of Indigenous and non-Indigenous persons attempting to work in sustainable cooperation with natural cycles, limits, and possibilities.*

This book takes a significant step in implementing relational interdisciplinary meanings of land-water management and sustainability (Berkes, 1999). It contributes on various intersections between land and water in different aspects of Indigenous life, particularly holistic meanings of people's lives and their environmental sustainability. Of special interest are, for instance, discourses and practices around the issue of environmental change, the local outcomes of various forms of resource conflicts (e.g., land or water entitlement), the environmental impact of rapid industrialization on Indigenous land and water, and the livelihood transitions taking place in response to globalized patterns of work and mobility. What kind of novel strategies for engaging with land and water do people develop/reutilize/ re-invent amid changing environmental sustainability? How do Indigenous, sustainable, traditional land-water management practices make sense of land-water policy-makers' transformation of land and water and its impact on their lives? In what ways (e.g., through spirituality, social, political, or other lenses) do they cope with the drastic, as well as long-term, modifications to their environment? To do this, this book attempts to contribute to understandings of how Indigenous communities understand and practice land-water management processes at the relational level of ontology – a level of awareness and being that continues to confound many who work in the environmental field (Nadasdy, 2007; Natcher & Clifford, 2007).

The book generates dialogue about relational ontology as it relates to Indigenous knowledge (IK), and it develops educational models that deepen understandings of IK from an ontological perspective. Through participatory action research (PAR), this book continues to unpack the social constructs (discourses) that may be preventing acknowledgment of, and thus authentic engagement with, underlying premises of IKs (Nadasdy, 2007). In developing a relational ontology, this book situates at the nexus of two pressing societal imperatives – the need for effective and ethical engagement with Indigenous peoples and their knowledges and mounting ecological crises – looking for ways to collaborate and interconnect these imperatives (Agrawal, 2002; Deloria, 1995).

The book critically engages scholarly debate between Western and Indigenous meanings of environmental resource *management* in relation to environmental sustainability, particularly in South Asian Indigenous territories (Aikenhead & Michell, 2011; Simpson, 2014). This book offers empirical evidence of how Western forms of management have remained unchanged in the neocolonial era, leaving numerous unjust forest development projects unchallenged in many parts of the world. This book claims that if Western management does not honor and/or consider Indigenous perspectives, significant consequences will result, including economic inequality, displacement, loss of traditional lifestyles, and significant environmental damage to the places and spaces associated with the many Indigenous communities around the world (Agrawal, 2002; Bohensky, E. L., & Maru, 2011; Escobar, 2008; Nadasdy, 2003). Furthermore, even today, indigenous scholars still do not feel comfortable fully articulating their ways of knowing (Watson, 2013), and knowledge gained through spiritual means is too often ignored or "scientized" to make it comprehensible to scientifically trained managers. If practices of sustainability are to successfully incorporate Indigenous knowledge, they must be based on shared understandings of relational ontologies and what De Sousa Santos calls "cognitive justice" (Coombes et al., 2012; Datta, 2015; Datta et al., 2014). This book advocates that alternative ways of protecting the Indigenous environment are not only ways of reconnecting; they are also the healing way for animals, people, forests, and so on. This book answers the following questions: How do South Asian Indigenous peoples view sustainability in relation to their own knowledge about the meanings of land and nature? How are governmental and transnational policies constructed within contested social and ecological landscapes? How can those of us who invoke the term sustainability most effectively address Indigenous ecological, economic, and social challenges? How do we create and enable conditions that lead to sustainability awareness and action while attending to the complex cultural variations existent in each circumstance? What are the meanings of research and researcher's responsibilities while conducting research with an Indigenous community? How is one to examine culture on its own if culture can be understood only in terms of the interactions among its many parts: its people, land, ideas, actions, and inactions, as well as its multiple pasts, presents, and futures? What are the underlying assumptions of sustainability theory and practice? To whom are we giving voice and agency, and at whose expense? Which forms of cultural knowledge and practice are privileged, and which forms are relegated to the margins? What are potentially unconventional routes for sustainability and research that will foster movement toward other ways of being?

This book argues that if Western forms of management do not honor and/or consider Indigenous perspectives as significant, it can lead to economic inequality, displacement, loss of traditional lifestyles, and significant environmental damage to the many Indigenous communities (Escobar, 2008; Nadasdy, 2003). Although each community has its own particular practices and ways of knowing, common to all indigenous traditions is a cosmology recognizing the potential of all beings to have forms of consciousness and spirit. Indigenous knowledges are based on a holistic, interconnected world where animals, plants, clouds, and other elements are animated and have the ability to communicate within and across land, water, and species, often across distance and time (Nadasdy, 2003). Given ongoing assumptions that Indigenous relations with nature are somehow "supernatural" or "extraordinary" (Cajete, 2000, p. 20), this book's disrupts the many ways in which traditional ecological knowledges continue to be viewed through dismissive Western lenses. Drawing from participatory action research (PAR) mythology, this book explores meanings of land-water management and sustainability with members of the Laitu Khyeng[1] Indigenous community in the Chittagong Hill Tracts (CHT), Bangladesh. This community, once isolated and thriving in its own way, is on the brink of extinction (Adnan, 2004). Traditionally, the Laitu Khyeng took care of extracting environmental resources without destroying the forest because sustaining it was necessary for their long-term survival (Adnan, 2004; Mohsin, 2002; Roy, 2000). However, according to Adnan (2004), Khyeng land-based rituals, practices, and traditional experiences, as well as its spiritually dominated sociopolitical structure, have been changing in recent years. These changes, which have been reported in various research studies as being due to government development projects and forest management policies, can be understood to be part of new land-based processes introduced through the nineteenth to twenty-first centuries during European colonization (Adnan, 2004). Despite the official end of colonization in 1947 across South Asia and in CHT, Bangladesh, people have continued to experience threats to their land rights, culture, and spirituality through government land-management, resettlement, displacement, development projects, and forest management policies (Mey, 1984; Thapa &

Rasul, 2006). This book explores the perspectives of community members on these two topics, including their understandings and rituals regarding land-water management and sustainability as directly connected to their currently precarious conditions. Therefore, this book examines how government land-management policies in the CHT affect traditional Indigenous practices with a particular focus on the Laitu Khyeng community in the region. Specifically: What were traditional Laitu Khyeng land-management customs and practices, particularly in relation to environmental sustainability? To what extent have Laitu Khyeng community members been affected by introduced land-water management policies? What are Laitu Khyeng hopes and expectations regarding land-management policies and practices, particularly in relation to environmental sustainability?

The reasons for writing this book

This book establishes a new interdisciplinary field of scholarly research supported by a relational network of community Elders, Knowledge-holders, scholars, students, activists, and professionals. This book contributes to: (1) identifying and challenging current environmental resource management problems on land-water, (2) generating further respect for Indigenous ways of knowing and relating to land-water, (3) studying societal responses to land-water stress, economics, and policy, (4) bridging between Indigenous and non-Indigenous researchers' understanding of the important role of Indigenous methodologies, ways of knowing, and environmental social justice.

This book improves the current practice of uncertainty treatment in land-water management by requiring better community participatory models. Yet understanding of what IK actually is and the words used to describe it (Battiste & Henderson, 2000; Dei, 2013; Cajete, 2000; McGregor, 2000) remain a topic of much debate (e.g., Houde, 2007; McGregor, 2000; Stuckey, 2010). The book advocates for understanding, respecting, and honoring IK, including consideration and communication of uncertainty. This book proposes to fill two significant gaps in intercultural communities of Indigenous and non-Indigenous management practices by: (1) developing methodological papers for the process of doing research together and offering a bridge between Indigenous and non-Indigenous practices, and (2) trying to answer the question or questions as determined by the Indigenous community.

This book takes a significant step in reclaiming and implementing Indigenous traditional practices in environmental resource management and sustainability (Berkes, 1999). It contributes to understandings of how Indigenous, non-Indigenous, governmental, nongovernmental organizations (NGO), environmental professionals, scholars, and activists can understand and practice resource management processes at the relational level of ontology – a level of awareness and being that continues to confound many who work in the environmental field (Nadasdy, 2007; Natcher & Clifford, 2007).

This book aims to fill various gaps in knowledge of the various Indigenous communities of Chittagong Hill Tracts (CHT), Bangladesh. In particular, this book examines Indigenous land alienation, the importance of local practices and traditional ways of land management, local ways of practicing sustainability, and the issues regarding existing governmental and nongovernmental land-management projects. In accordance with the research questions, this book was guided by a critical concern for identifying the problems with existing land-management practices and policies and for finding ways to frame the Laitu Khyeng community's meanings of sustainability as they relate to their everyday land-management practices and traditional experiences of management. The book situates itself within this context and represents a significant step in exploring identity and justice in relation to Indigenous understandings of land management (Tuck & McKenzie, 2016).

The book aims to make a contribution to both research and practice in ways that benefit the participants in the hopes of inspiring a new culture of sustainability in Indigenous regions, particularly in the Laitu Khyeng community (McKenzie et al., 2009). For example, participants articulated diverse cultural practices related to environmental issues and solutions, demonstrated relationships to their environment and their ancestral land and water, found opportunities to document their traditional experiences with their environment, and shared their knowledge with each other.

This book also continues to unpack the social constructs (discourses) that may be preventing acknowledgment of, and thus authentic engagement with, underlying premises of Indigenous knowledges (Nadasdy, 2007). This book demonstrates effective and ethical engagement with Indigenous peoples and their knowledge in solving ecological crises. The project models intercultural collaboration and ways to work across "disparate and irreconcilable systems of thought" (Barnhardt & Kawagley, 2003, n.p.), which cannot simply be integrated one into the other (Agrawal, 2002; Deloria, 1995).

This book significantly tries to redefine the meanings of research and researcher from the participants' perspectives, particularly from perspectives of the Indigenous community's Elders, Knowledge-holders, leaders, and youth. I understand that research involving Indigenous peoples in many Indigenous communities has been defined and carried out primarily by non-Indigenous academics and researchers (Dei, 2011; Kovach, 2009; Smith, 2008). Indigenous and non-Indigenous scholars who are working with Indigenous communities (Berkes, 2009; Nadasdy, 2003; Wilson, 2008) argue that Western approaches and non-Indigenous scholars have not generally reflected Indigenous worldviews, and the research and researchers have not necessarily benefited Indigenous peoples or communities. As a result, these people continue to regard research, particularly research originating outside their communities, with a certain apprehension or mistrust. For instance, during this book's field research, one of the knowledge-holders, Kasamong Pure Khyeng from the Laitu community in CHT, explained how research could be exploitation if both researcher and research did not originate in the participants' community:

> Many researchers have been using our community people, our culture, and knowledge to do business. For example, lots of student researchers get their

academic degree through using our knowledge; lots of university and research institute researchers have been making money by using our traditional knowledge; lots of NGOs have been getting money from various donor agencies by selling our traditional knowledge. What have we gotten from these university student researchers, university and research institute researchers, and NGO and government researchers? I have not seen any benefit from these researchers and their research for me, my community, and our culture. I see the term *research* is as a business making use of our community's people, culture, and practice. We are fearful when we hear the word *research*. It takes our time, knowledge, and practice for other people's business, and we do not get anything from it; we do not even know what knowledge has been taken or how it has been used. All we get is a couple of drinks [tea/coffee]. We do not want this kind of research in our community. We are so disappointed in any kind of research nowadays. We have not seen any findings from many of the researchers. Researchers take our knowledge that we shared as friends; they use our knowledge for their discoveries, funding, and academic degrees. We helped many researchers in many ways so that they could get the proper information that they were looking for; however, the researchers did not give us anything.

On a similar issue, another Indigenous Elder asked us why they should participate in these exploitative forms of research. She said (anonymous added):

Now that you are planning to do research with us, I would like to know what kinds of benefits we [as a community] will get from your research. Will we get any benefits from your research at all? We need to know how you as a researcher and your research can be useful to our community. Can you promise us that you will not be like previous researchers? We want promises from you and from your research before we get involved with your research. We would also like to know how you are going to use our knowledge. Who will be the owner of our knowledge?

There are other important, challenging issues motivating this book, such as how both our research and we as researchers need to transform from our Western form of research and researcher to a participant-oriented research and researcher.

This book's journey was not easy; however, I consider this book's research as a journey of ceremony (Wilson, 2008), which not only forced me to rethink my research but also challenged who we are as researchers and our responsibilities as researchers. This book suggests that the meanings of research and researchers are the continuous forms of transformation of the participants and the participant community's needs. The term *transformation* refers to forms of becoming and taking responsibility for participants. This book explains how research and researcher transformation happens. One of the hopes of this book is to inspire other researchers to transform for their research participants.

This book promotes Indigenous traditional knowledge of how to live sustainably and challenges the Western management processes, formal education systems, and governmental and nongovernmental development policies that have disrupted the practical everyday aspects of Indigenous knowledge and ways of learning, replacing them with non-Indigenous, academic ways of learning. A number of studies (Agrawal, 2002; Bohensky & Maru, 2011; Escobar, 2013, 2008; Nadasdy, 2003) suggest the grave risk that much Indigenous knowledge is being lost and, along with it, valuable knowledge about ways of living sustainably. This book takes a political stand for Indigenous ways of understanding management through traditional Indigenous ways of knowing, practicing, and informing cultivation culture in their land that are reflections of environmental sustainability (Dudgeon & Berkes, 2003).

This book also challenges the increase in human-generated environmental damage, recognizes prior and continuing wrongs against Indigenous peoples and inappropriate use of their knowledge, and takes a closer look at fundamental assumptions governing past decisions. It takes a critical step toward reorganizing and including Indigenous knowledge and practice in informing policy options that address land and water uncertainty and impediments to effective land and water governance for developing sustainable environmental management strategies while potentially offering a significant bridge between Western and Indigenous ways of environmental resource management and sustainability.

There are multiple other reasons for writing this book: finding meanings for research and researcher, centering local Indigenous perspectives on their traditional land-water sustainability practices, and challenging Western epistemology of management that has spread in the wake of colonialism and the capitalist economic system, excluding and Othering Indigenous knowledge in their own land.

Why Indigenous sustainability?

Meanings of Indigenous environmental sustainability have been either misunderstood or misrepresented by both the Bangladeshi government and nongovernmental organizations in CHT. The political history of the region begins with the history of "modern" forestry in this area. During colonial rule (1757–1947), the British marked the CHT as a spatially distinctive ecological region and declared the whole area forest in 1865. More recently, the CHT Indigenous areas have become a site of political struggle for identities, power, and control over resources and lands, leading to an armed struggle between the Bangladeshi armed forces and the Chittagong Hill Tracts People's United Party (a regional party in CHT). The state's ecological exploitation has come to dominate traditional ways of learning and doing through the government and nongovernmental organizations' sustainability implications, including the privatization of Indigenous lands and forests and displacement, all of which are partly enabled through mainstream forest management, development, and essential educational processes (Adnan, 2004; Schendel et al., 2001). Recently, Indigenous communities' traditional cultivation practices and learning process have negatively changed as a result of the state's misunderstandings of Indigenous environmental sustainability. In addition, misconceptions

8 *Introduction*

about Indigenous sustainability are embedded within the state's environmental assessment and policies in CHT (Chakma, 2010).

The CHT land includes thirteen Indigenous groups (Chapola, 2008) and the Khyeng community, particularly Laitu Khyeng, is one of the most affected and vulnerable communities in terms of access to land-water rights and traditional cultivation practices, as well as in relation to the government and NGOs' plant-privatization processes, militarization, settlement, and administrative oppressions and discriminations (Datta & Chapola, 2007). Moreover, Bangladeshi government and transnational bodies' development projects' environmental management practices and mainstream environmental education have misrepresented the CHT (Adnan, 2004) and have resulted in increased environmental and cultural vulnerability.

Centering *Indigenous perspectives on environmental sustainability* through Indigenous customs and experiences will potentially benefit many communities and allow them to engage in diverse sustainability practices and solutions in CHT and beyond. This book's main goal is to promote the next generation of environmental researcher, educators, and policy-makers in Bangladesh and South Asia at a deeper and heightened level of understandings on Indigenous land-water management and sustainability. Through the acknowledgment, respect, honor, and application of Indigenous perspectives with non-Indigenous knowledge systems in environmental sustainability, a strong new relationship will emerge between Indigenous and non-Indigenous peoples.

Land-Water Management and Sustainability in Bangladesh: Indigenous Practices in the Chittagong Hill Tracts an invitation for all of us to work together as indigenists to build relational networks to the important work of creating an intercultural bridge, moving beyond cultural awareness and inclusion, and challenging racist ideology as we rethink and reimagine ourselves in relationship with one another sharing a place – a motherland (Battiste, 2013; Wilson, 2013).

Readers

Indigenous environmental sustainability is a growing field throughout the world. In addition, Indigenous traditional practices have created major positive impacts in Bangladesh, South Asia, and internationally. *Land-Water Management and Sustainability in Bangladesh* will be of interest to academic specialists studying environmental conservation and policy-making considerations in Bangladesh, South Asia, Asia, Australia, New Zealand, Norway, and South and North America. Yet, often, for many reasons, the Indigenous and environmental agendas do not coincide, particularly in the South Asian Indigenous region.

Putting aside the contrary historical record – when European colonizers plundered Indigenous lands, exterminating the herds of animals, damming the water sources, and felling the forests – the supposedly heightened environmental consciousness of modern Western societies has not necessarily assuaged Indigenous peoples. The history of Indigenous environmental sustainability in South Asia provides one of the first hints that a vast chasm can arise between Western environmental policies and the interests of local communities. By foregrounding ethical research relationships and focusing on issues of ontology (understandings of reality), which govern significant aspects of relational ontology (Datta et al., 2015), this research enables more effective dialogue within and across Indigenous communities to safeguard environmental sustainability and support greater social justice through Indigenous knowledge.

This research benefits many people: environmental students, faculty, researchers, activists, environmental professionals, and anyone who works with landwater management policies. It also provides particular value to Indigenous peoples, who, up to this point in time, have had to spend inordinate amounts of time "teaching" Western-trained educators, professionals, and citizens about their basic understandings of the world before the knowledge they bring to the table could be understood and valued. Although my initial focus is on Laitu communities in Chittagong Hill Tracts (CHT), Bangladesh, I anticipate this research to be of high interest to those working in South Asia and other Indigenous communities in Asia and beyond.

This book may useful to critical readers in environmental sociology, anthropology, interdisciplinary studies, postcolonial studies, ethnic studies, environmental sustainability, South Asian studies, and Indigenous and women's studies. Because this book could not be produced without building upon and working within a number of fields including postcolonial theories, Indigenous methodologies and methods, sustainability theory and practices, Asian studies, political economics, youth practice, Indigenous knowledge and practice, this book will also appeal to different disciplinary, interdisciplinary, and transdisciplinary academics and practitioners. Because this book tries to demonstrate what Indigenous scholar Linda Smith calls a "decolonization and reclaiming approach," it will also be relevant to the policy-making community in both the Eastern and Western world.

Land-Water Management and Sustainability in Bangladesh Indigenous Practices in the Chittagong Hill Tracts also provides a fresh and extensive discussion in environmental sustainability sectors. Reflecting on recent debates in management research and revisiting resource management challenges in light of political ecology approaches, this book provides a series of nuanced and policy-relevant chapters analyzing patterns of management around natural resources and options to reach environmental sustainability goals.

This forward-thinking book is essential reading for students and academics in the fields of development studies, anthropology, political ecology, environmental sociology, environmental education, human geography, development economics, and international political economy. The evidence and policy solutions included will be of great appeal to policy-makers and practitioners.

A note about terminology

Throughout this book, the term *Laitu* refers to the Khyeng Indigenous people, particularly those who have been living in three villages (i.e., Gungru Para, Gungru Mukh Para, and Gunru Modrom Para) in the Bandarban district in CHT,

Bangladesh. Two clans exist within the Khyeng community: the Laitu Khyeng and the Kantu Khyeng. The Laitu Khyeng mostly live in the flat land, and the Kantu Khyeng community mostly live in hilly land. The Kantu Khyeng people live mostly in Keplang para and Arachori para in the Rangamati district in CHT. The Laitu and Kongtu Khyeng peoples have many similarities in terms of culture, language, food, and cloths; however, the Laitu Khyeng people are more affected by the mainstream colonization (see Chapter 1 for more information).

The meanings of the term *Western* are ontologically contradictory to Indigenous understanding of environment in many Indigenous communities' worldviews, practices, and methods (Dudgeon & Berkes, 2003). The Western and Indigenous ideas of environment carry fundamentally different meanings in terms of different worldviews with their own philosophy, practices, and methods (Lertzman, 2010; Lertzman & Vredenburg, 2005). Western understanding/knowledge of environment is as a technique to be not only incorporated but also oppressed into Indigenous understanding/knowledge of management (Nadasdy, 1999). North American environmental anthropologist Nadasdy (1999) also suggests that the Western meaning of environment "takes for granted existing power relations between aboriginal people and the state by assuming that traditional knowledge is simply a new form of 'data' to be incorporated into already existing management bureaucracies" (p. 15). First Nation scholars Battiste and Henderson (2000) suggest that attempts to define traditional ecological knowledge (i.e., environment) are inherently colonial, based on a Eurocentric need to categorize and control. The concept of management has not changed from colonial perspectives in the neocolonial era, leaving numerous unjust forest development projects unchallenged in many parts of the world (Nadasdy, 2011, 2003; Escobar, 2008, 1995). If Western environment does not honor and/or consider Indigenous perspectives as significant, it can lead to economic inequality, displacement, loss of traditional lifestyles, and significant environmental damage to the many Indigenous communities will follow (Escobar, 2008; Nadasdy, 2003).

The term *decolonization* is used throughout this book without contradictions. As Tuck and Yang (2012) have argued, the term *decolonization* is a special word, often conflated with anticolonial projects and struggles that reinscribe the logics of settler colonialism, in particular the reoccupation of Indigenous lands. In this way, for the purposes of this book, I define *decolonization* as anticolonial struggle that grows out of the participants' perspectives.

The term *neocolonial* is used to describe new forms of colonization that are perpetuated through globalized trade, as well as existing, ongoing colonial practices related to the development model and land management (Escobar, 2010).

The term *Indigenous* is used as a knowledge consciousness arising locally and in association with a long-term occupancy of a place (Dei, 2002). This term is used to mean those who have a distinct language, culture, customary laws, and social and political institutions that are different from the dominant ethnolinguistic group in South Asia (IWGIA, 2010).

The term *we* refers collectively to the research team and the collective ways of conducting research as part of participatory action research (PAR) (Datta et al.,

2015). The term includes a university researcher and community participants (Elders, Knowledge-holders, leaders, and four coresearcher participants). We, as a collective research team, were continuously engaged and participated all through the field research and data analysis processes, such as identifying research questions; facilitating traditional sharing circles; conducting participant observation and photovoice; recording traditional sharing circles and individual storytelling discussions; maintaining a commonplace book, which was used to record personal observations, art, poems, experiences, stories about the environment, and field notes; and helping with coding and analyzing research data (Datta et al., 2015).

The word *colonial* refers in this book to a practice of domination, which involves the subjugation of one people by another. The term draws attention to the way that one group/country/person exercises power over another, whether through control through settlement, sovereignty, grabbing and using Indigenous land, and/or indirect mechanisms of control.

The word *antiessential* is used to describe a process of rejection of any permanent meaning. It is a process of recognizing various forms of knowing (Escobar, 1999).

The words *Elders* and *Knowledge-holders* are capitalized throughout this book as a symbol of respect and honor for the community. Elders often provide the wisdom, knowledge, and ceremonial guidance to assist with research processes that respect Indigenous worldviews. Elders have a special role to play in this research. The community looks to them for guidance and sound judgment. They are recognized for their wisdom, their stability, their humor, and their ability to know what is appropriate in particular land-water management and sustainability situations. They are the vigorous source of a community's sustainability in multiple ways.

- Know traditional teachings and are committed to helping people within this framework;
- Are physically, emotionally, mentally, and spiritually healthy;
- Are born with, or seek, the gift of healing in apprenticeship with a traditional healer;
- Walk their talk, that is, live a healthy lifestyle within the parameters of traditional values;
- Provide help when asked, although may not provide this immediately (will sometimes refer to another Elder with particular expertise);
- Have the ability to bring traditional values and life ways into contemporary urban life and living in a practical way;
- Treat their family, spouse, children, parents, Elders, and other traditional healers in a respectful and caring manner [all people];
- Serve as a positive role model for the Indigenous community's future generations;
- Can teach and correct behavior with traditional culture and respect without humiliating the individual;
- Are always hopeful and able to see the goodness in people; and
- Know the medicines and ceremonies.

12 *Introduction*

The term *minority* is used to indicate non-Islamic minority communities, including religious minority communities (e.g., Hindu, Buddhist, Christian), as well as various Indigenous minority communities (Human Right Report, 2014). The academic researcher (Datta) was born in a family that belonged to a religious (Hindu) minority family. Both religious and Indigenous minority communities have often had to face many difficulties in attaining equal land rights, equal policy-making authority, and equal education rights in Bangladesh (Human Right Report, 2014). Many communities have been displaced from their original land, oppressed in their everyday practices, and excluded from any kind of major decision-making processes in relation to their land (Internal Displacement Monitoring Centre Report, 2018; Iva, 2010).

Traditional Indigenous land-water management practices refers to the indigenous community's past, present, and future practices. It is a continuous and ongoing process.

The word *meanings* refers to the participant community's perceptions, views, perspectives, understandings, and interpretations of their everyday traditional knowledge, interactions, and communication with land-water management (Datta, 2015; Thompson, 2013).

Research context

This research was set within the Chittagong Hill Tracts (CHT) area of Bangladesh. With an area of approximately 5,089 square miles in the southeastern part of Bangladesh, the CHT covers 10% of the land in the country and is divided into three districts: Bandarban in the south, Khagrachari in the north, and Rangamathi in the center. All three districts differ from the rest of Bangladesh due to their mountainous and forested landscape, ethnic composition, and cultural and spiritual lifestyle (Adnan, 2004; Chowdhury, 2008). The CHT was originally inhabited by diverse groups of Indigenous communities (Adnan & Dastidar, 2011; Roy, 2000), although there is disagreement regarding the number of these original Indigenous communities and the naming of current Indigenous communities in the CHT (Chowdhury, 2008). Indigenous communities identified in the literature include the *Tanchangya, Tripura, Pankha, Marma, Mru, Lushai, Khumi, Khyeng, Chak, Chakma, Bawm, Santal, Rakhin, Gurkha,* and *Ahomia* (Adnan, 2004). The Laitu Khyeng (Figure 1.1) is one of these indigenous communities in the CHT region of Bangladesh and is the main focus of this book.

A number of common practices and values existed in the Indigenous communities prior to colonization. For example, before the mid-1700s, political power in CHT Indigenous communities, including the Laitu Khyeng, operated through traditional culture and customs. Land management had been maintained through the communities' spiritual relationships and traditional experiences (Schendel et al., 2001). The people had close relationships with the land, animals, and plants; they were thought of as protection from a food crisis and as members of the greater community (Mey, 1984).

However, colonization changed much in the CHT community. Colonization initially occurred in Bangladesh via British imperial rule in 1757, formally ending almost 200 years later in 1947. Colonialism, Mohsin (1997) argues, became a powerful actor in defining Indigenous people's lives through discriminatory state-development models, such as reserve forests, commercial logging, and the act of giving outsiders access to Indigenous land. Such models gave theoretical and practical tools to the colonizers or developers to maintain the oppressive situations to their advantage. For example, in the 1860s the British first occupied the CHT, taking power away from Indigenous communities (Schendel et al., 2001). The land-management policies imposed by the British state were aggressive toward the CHT Indigenous communities (Adnan, 2004) and introduced what Schendel et al. (2001) call the first "colonial" stage affecting traditional land-management practices (p. 3). Several other studies (e.g., Adnan, 2004) explain that the CHT Indigenous land was first opened to businesspersons from outside the CHT through British-controlled land-management policies initiated by the colonial British state to encourage investment and use of Indigenous lands for profitable purposes. Similarly, Roy (2000) shows that the British development models and forest-management policies led to the use of Indigenous forest land for business, which challenged Indigenous communities' traditional cultural practices. During the period of British rule, the region studied in this research project was formally named the Chittagong Hill Tracts. According to Schendel et al. (2001) and Adnan (2004), the British decided to recruit three Indigenous leaders for this region for two main reasons: to be able to use CHT land and to collect taxes from Indigenous people. As Mohsin (2002) and Roy (2000) explain, the implementation of British government taxation policies served to undermine the Indigenous traditional administrative structure and management practices.

Indigenous traditional land-water management practices faced more challenges in neocolonial nation-states, such as Pakistan, 1947–1971, and Bangladesh, 1972-present, as well as those that have been more recently impacted through practices and structures of economic globalization (Adnan, 2004; Roy, 2000). Bangladesh and Pakistan can thus be viewed as a neocolonial states, by which I mean the current colonial attitudes that these nation-state governments have toward CHT Indigenous communities in Bangladesh such that colonial land-management policies are ongoing (Adnan, 2004; Roy, 2000). Neocolonial states, Schendel et al. (2001) explicitly argue, have ignored traditional Indigenous land-management policies and have marginalized and suppressed CHT Indigenous people and kept them from their land rights. Similarly, Mohsin (1997) thinks that colonialism has not yet ended in the CHT; rather, it has taken on new forms of exploitation. Through various forms of exploitation, such as land grabbing, displacement, and imposing dominant education and language on Indigenous communities, the Pakistani and Bangladeshi nation states continue to perpetuate colonial imperialism in CHT Indigenous communities (Adnan, 2004; Nath & Inoue, 2009). These impacts continue to affect land rights, traditional practices, and culture across Indigenous communities in CHT Bangladesh (Adnan, 2004). To stress the point, Roy (1996) explains that these neocolonial states have not only given land entitlement to outsiders, they have also introduced various uneven development programs on CHT Indigenous land.

Studies by Adnan and Dastidar (2011), Mey (1984), and Roy (2000) show that the neocolonial states' land- and forest-management policies have also had far-reaching effects on Indigenous culture. For instance, these policies have been contributing factors in the separation of Indigenous people from their relationships with organisms (including animals, birds, plants, parasites, and fish), spirituality (including natural law, feelings, and respect), and physical reality (including land and local mode of production) (Berkes, 2009). According to a number of studies (e.g., Adnan & Dastidar, 2011; Chapola, 2008; Mey, 1984; Roy, 2000), the Laitu Khyeng community, like other Indigenous communities in CHT, has been affected by colonial and neocolonial states' land-management policies. Adnan (2004) argues that the Laitu Khyeng community is the most alienated Indigenous community in Bangladesh, in part due to being one of the poorest in CHT. Adnan (2004), Chakma (2010), and Roy (2000) explicitly argue that there is a need to promote Indigenous land-management practices in government projects in ways that protect Indigenous land rights, culture, identity, and ecosystems.

Though traditional practices have been changing due to colonial and neocolonial state land-management approaches, Indigenous communities' traditional practices are still known and used in the cultivation of the land for domestic purposes (Roy, 2000, p. 54). For example, most CHT Indigenous communities still continue to be economically dependent on their traditional cultivation practices, such as fishing, trapping, and gathering, within their land and forest (Adnan, 2004). These forms of land use have been traditionally distributed and managed by Indigenous leaders known as Chiefs, Head (men-women-others), and *Karbari* (village head) (Roy, 2000).

The context set out here exemplifies the need to study traditional Indigenous land-management practices and critically exploring existing government land-management policies and their expectations and hopes for future land-management policies. Existing research on Indigenous communities in the subcontinent, especially in the CHT, has mostly been based on either government documents or development frameworks. Government documents tend to ignore Indigenous traditional culture and customs, while according to Jashimuddin and Inoue (2012) and Adnan (2004), development studies are mainly concerned with governmental and nongovernmental economic interests. Roy (2000) also argues that the literature often overlooks colonial and neocolonial nation-states and multinational agencies' marginalizing attitudes toward Indigenous communities in CHT. Such literature often justifies development models over Indigenous traditional practices, such as the Karnafully Paper Mill project in 1953 and the Kapati Dam in 1957, not to mention favoring the interests of tobacco companies and commercial plantations (1972–present), resettlement policies (1975–1985), and commercial companies. Debnath (2010) also states that Indigenous traditional and spiritual practices are mostly ignored in these economic, profit-based project processes. Similarly, Banerjee (2000) explains that the mainstream literature is ignorant of the ongoing brutality toward Indigenous people's land rights and traditional practices. This book aims to critically explore existing development projects and policies in relation to Laitu Khyeng Indigenous land-management practices.

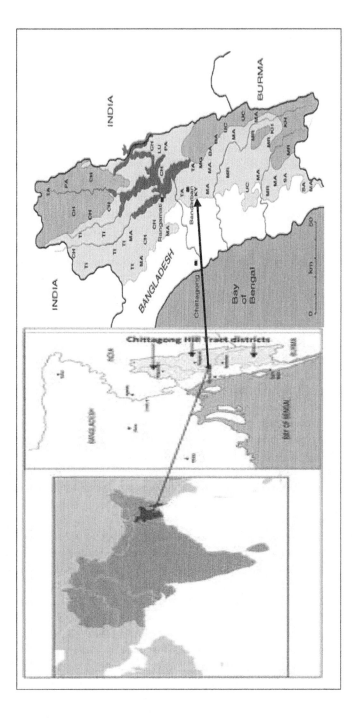

Figure 1.1 CHT map: *Map of Indigenous communities and Laitu Khyeng indigenous communities in CHT, Bangladesh.* This figure represents Indigenous communities in CHT, Bangladesh: BA – Bawm, CH – Chakma, KH – Khumi, **KY – Khyeng (Laitu Khyeng)**, LU – Lushai, MA – Marma, UC – Uchay, MR – Mru, PA – Pankho, SA – Sak, and TA – Tanchangya.

Source: Indigenous Work Groups of Indigenous Affairs (IWGIA), Retrieved March 8, 2018, from www.iwgia.org/regions/asia/the-chittagong-hill-tracts.

Ethnic diversity in CHT

In this section, I describe Bandarban District's ethnic composition and its changing patterns. The aim is not to provide a comprehensive and rigorous analysis of Bandarban District's ethnic diversity. Rather, this focus helps to bring out distinctive features of the Laitu Khyeng Indigenous villages in terms of their living conditions and social and economic activities.

Historically the Bandarban District in Chittagong Hill Tracts (CHT), including the Marma, Chama, Bawm, Tanchanghya, and Mru Indigenous communities, has been ethnically diverse. This diverse ethnic composition is important for multiple environmental activities, such as traditional Jhum and plains land cultivation, livestock and poultry raising, fruit growing, hunting and gathering, fishing, spinning, and weaving, and craft work. However, this ethnic composition has been changing rapidly and coming under serious threat due to a number of critical factors and events. For example, studies (e.g., Adnan, 2004; Ahmed, 2012; Chakma, 2010; Roy, 1996) have identified influential economic activities introduced by Bangali settlers following transmigration as well as by government departments, development agencies, and private-sector businesses of local, national, and foreign origins. Evidence shows that these factors have been damaging the Bandarban district's ethnic diversity.

The Laitu Khyeng community's villages are interconnected with other Indigenous communities' villages, including Marma, Bawm, Tanchainghya, and Mru communities. Although these Indigenous communities' languages, cultures, and celebrations are varied and uneven in terms of content, they complement each other in many respects (Chakma, 2010). The varied ethnic composition also highlights the diversity of environmental, cultural, and economic land-management practices in the Bandarban district (Chapola, 2008). Loffler's (1991) study with the CHT Indigenous community shows that the sharing of practices among communities upholds belongingness and traditional cultivation cultures. Adnan (2011, 2004) also explains that such sharing of cultivation practices in the Laitu Khyeng community builds a "sense of community based on the consideration that the inhabitations of the village have, so to speak, grown up together and share a common culture" (Adnan, 2004, p. 68).

The diverse ethnic composition in Bandarban District leads to peaceful living conditions for the Indigenous communities. For example, the boundary is defined by the actual location of a cluster of households, which the members of the various Indigenous communities acknowledge as a shared village community. Such mutual living and cultivation approaches are socially and culturally accepted practices (Adnan, 2004). Diverse ethnic composition in Bandarban District can be understood as a form of unity for the Indigenous communities in the area.

Although this diverse ethnic composition is important for Indigenous land-management practices and culture, the shared traditional land-management practices are under threat from illegal settlement activities. As evident from the data on ethnic composition, in 1872 the Bandarban District's ethnic diversity included Marma (40%), Mru (20%), Tanchonga (10%), other Indigenous groups (Khyeng,

Mru, and Bawn) (28%), and Bangali (2%). In 1991, the Bandarban District's demographic became Bangali (52%), Marma (26%), Tripura (4%), Tanchonga (2%), Mru (10%), Khyeng (1%), and Bawn (3%) (Adnan, 2004). According to Roy (1996) the Bandarban District's ethnic diversity has been drastically reduced during the internal displacement of the postcolonial period (Pakistan 1947–1971 and Bangladesh 1972–current). Many indigenous communities' displacement has been caused by "acts of violence as well as their [Indigenous] changing survival needs" (Adnan, 2004, p. 54). Another example from the national newspaper (Prothom Alo, 2015) shows that the profitable Bangali-owned Brickfield Company is forcefully trying to break peaceful, diverse ethnic relationships in the Laitu Khyeng community. The article also reports that this project has brought more than 1,000 Bangali migrant workers into the Laitu Khyeng community within the last ten years.

These recent changes have been challenging the peaceful and sustainable ethnic composition in Bandarban District (Roy, 1996). Therefore, Adnan (2004) and Chapola (2008) clearly state that recent migration and development projects are not only endangering the Laitu Khyeng Indigenous community's sustainable and relational practices with others diverse ethnic communities but also have led to the Laitu community being one of the poorest Indigenous communities in Bandarban District, with a general lack of access to land and water.

Theoretical framework, methodology, and methods

Using the conceptual framework of a relational ontology, this research examines meanings of land-management and sustainability such as traditional experiences, culture, and customs, which are important issues for Indigenous lives and the environment (Datta, 2015). A relational ontology invokes a collaboration of ontologies that come from people's everyday culture and practices (Datta, 2015). It deconstructs our pre-existing ideas of land management and implicitly leaves behind all prioritizations that contain a modern dualistic source (Datta et al., 2014a). A relational ontology also focuses on the researcher's relational accountability and obligations to the study's participants and research site (Datta et al., 2015; Wilson, 2008, 2007).

To complement a relational theoretical framework, I used a participatory action research (PAR) methodology. PAR has been used in other research to foster change through community-based participation, building off participants' everyday local practices, culture, and relational and spiritual knowledge (Datta et al., 2015). Five methods of data collection were used. These included traditional sharing circles (TSC) used for sharing land-management experiences and expectations in the community. Individual story sharing was used for deeper understanding of land management and sustainability from participants' personal experiences. Photovoice was used to explore relational and spiritual land-management stories. Commonplace books (Sumara, 1996) were used for collecting personal experiences and feelings regarding introduced land-management practices. Finally, participant observation was used for understanding and interpreting the participants' expressions and responses.

Limitations of this book

This book was limited to the Laitu Indigenous community from the Bandarban District (one of the CHT areas) but did not include another Khyeng Indigenous community (Kantu Khyeng from the Rangamathi District in CHT). I have chosen this Laitu community because I have been professionally and emotionally involved with it for the last fifteen years and actively engaged with Indigenous and minority land, water, and education rights movements in the area. As a result, I had a formal and informal working knowledge of contacts and protocols for working with the Laitu Khyeng in the CHT.

My focus was specifically on local ways of approaching issues in the Laitu Khyeng villages and may carry with it certain assumptions of the community it is embedded in. Therefore, results cannot be generalized. In terms of research participants, the research was restricted to Laitu Indigenous participants (i.e., Elders, Knowledge-holders, leaders, youth participants), and they were selected based on the Elders' and Knowledge-holders' recommendations. Perhaps other participants who were not included would have provided different views and perspectives; however, during our results presentation to the community, other community members participated.

Another limitation concerns viewing myself as an insider/outsider. I was treated as an insider throughout the research process due to my minority identity and personal relationships with the community. However, I was not able to speak the local language and had to depend on coresearcher participants' translations. Because I do not come from this community and I cannot speak the Laitu language, I lacked the knowledge of how the community interacts and relates to each other and whether any political and power issues exist within and across the tribes. If I were a native member of the community, perhaps I would have had different insights.

Outline of the book chapters

This introductory chapter addresses the overall research questions and perspectives of this book and introduces key findings from the research. This chapter introduces why research is important in protecting ethnic diversity and advocating for an Indigenous culture and practice. It introduces the context of the book by describing the effects of colonialism and neocolonialism in the CHT (and in the Laitu Khyeng Indigenous community in particular) in relation to land management in the area. As defined by the indigenous Elders, Knowledge-holders, leaders, and coresearcher participants, this book offers insight into specific indicators of Indigenous perspectives for those who will either use it or be in a position to assess its use. This book takes the form of four layers or dimensions: (1) the research's relational theoretical framework (Chapter 2); (2) situating researcher and research (Chapter 3); (3) Indigenous perspectives on land-water management and sustainability (Chapters 4, 5, and 6); and (4) research in action (Chapters 7, 8, and 9).

Introduction 19

Chapter 2 – Relational theoretical framework and implications for land, management, and sustainability: This chapter focuses on what may be achieved through taking up the complex exploration of nature, land, and sustainability and is a growing field of inquiry in both science and social science, particularly for those who are interested in the local environment. Meanings of nature, land, and sustainability have been either misunderstood or misrepresented within disciplinary boundaries in many Indigenous communities. To explore the meanings of things such as nature, land, and sustainability in these communities, we as researchers had better first acknowledge the spirituality and local experiences that connect one actor with other actors. A relational ontology is the conceptual framework within which I suggest meanings for traditional land, nature, and sustainability, such as traditional experiences, culture, and customs that are important issues for Indigenous lives and the environment. This framework may potentially guide the researcher through the critical concerns of identifying the problems of existing land, nature, and sustainability management in relation to the everyday land-based practices and traditional experiences in Indigenous regions.

Chapter 3 – Participatory action research and researcher responsibilities: This chapter seeks to explore the relational participatory action research (PAR) frameworks that have been developed to allow non-Indigenous researchers, along with Indigenous coresearcher participants, to learn and honor Indigenous stories. Specifically, in the context of PAR research in the Chittagong Hill Tracts of Bangladesh, I outline: (a) potential challenges between Indigenous research paradigms and Western research paradigms, (b) the situation of the non-Indigenous researcher in relation to the Indigenous community, (c) challenges associated with the non-Indigenous researcher's selection of a research site, (d) collaboration throughout the research process, and (e) the processes of developing and maintaining responsibilities. The aim is not to offer simple answers to such challenges but to highlight the manner in which such processes can be addressed. This chapter may provide practical insight for future non-Indigenous researchers working with Indigenous communities through a participatory sharing process with Indigenous coresearcher participants, Elders, leaders, Knowledge-holders, and youth.

Chapter 4 – Traditional meanings of land-water: Amid ongoing, contemporary colonialism, this chapter discusses the important of Indigenous perspectives on traditional land-water customs and practices in their sustainabilities. The purpose of this chapter is to find ways to protect land-water, encourage the sharing of traditional knowledge when appropriate, enhance community education, and assist in land-water management and policy development. I conclude this chapter by advocating for Indigenous meanings of land-water due to its effectiveness in guiding policy-makers and researchers to develop robust governance for Indigenous knowledge integration in land-water management.

Chapter 5 – The community's perceptions of meanings of management: This chapter answers some key challenges that face us today: What can Western science learn from traditional land-water management? How can we bridge between

Western and Indigenous land-water management? Do we have within us the necessary wisdom and knowledge to make this happen? To answer these questions, this chapter focuses on exploring the meanings of land-water and management from Indigenous people's everyday lives and their natural resource embodiment.

Chapter 6 – The community's perceptions of current management: This chapter discusses one of the main research questions of this book: To what extent were the community members affected by introduced land- and forest-management practices, such as those promoted by the government, NGOs, commercial companies, and multinational corporations? Three subthemes emerge from participants' stories: the first centers on the community's perceptions of current management projects (governmental and nongovernmental agencies' land-, water-, and forest-management projects); the second details the projects themselves, contrasting external administrative tenets with traditional Indigenous practices (specifically, the commercial Brickfield industrial company project, the for-profit tobacco plantation project, the wood-plants plantation and reserve forest projects); and the third illuminates visible and invisible consequences of the above-mentioned land-management projects, including effects impacting women and species populations. The following section discusses the above three themes and their impacts in relation to community perceptions.

Chapter 7 – The community's perceptions of environmental sustainability: This chapter examines how an Indigenous community understands sustainability and analyzes these understandings in relation to the literature on the politics of nature as well as Indigenous and postcolonial studies. Particular emphasis is given to Indigenous worldviews, spiritual and relational practices, culture, lands, and revitalization.

Chapter 8 – Youth responsibilities for sustainability: This chapter traces a model of epistemic empowerment of Indigenous youth through their hopes, dreams, and responsibilities for sustainability. This chapter is organized across eight categories: (i) meanings of sustainability to youth, (ii) youth's hopes and dreams for building sustainability, (iii) fostering critical imagination and analytical skills, (iv) strengthening connections with local culture, (v) learning Indigenous cultivations skills, (vi) breaking the culture of silence, (vii) embracing ethically and socially responsible educational knowledge, and (viii) encountering resistance in applying emancipatory ideas.

Chapter 9 – A call to implications: guiding principles for environmental sustainability: This chapter discusses Indigenous sustainability perspectives by focusing on policy and practice. This chapter's discussion is centered on four main topics in relation to the Laitu Khyeng Indigenous community's natural resource management and sustainability: the meaning of land and water, the understanding and practices of management, the impact of colonialism, and the community's imagined goals in pursuit of sustainability. This chapter includes a commentary on the implications of the research for policy and practice and suggestions for future research. This chapter ends with the researcher's personal reflections on the process of conducting this collective study.

Chapter 10 – Concluding remarks: I conclude this introduction with a note about the political position of this book. This research is committed to advocating for traditional environmental culture, practices, and ancestral knowledge and both challenges and contributes to existing knowledge of Indigenous peoples' land stewardship while preserving information that might otherwise have been lost. It is about rethinking land-water management and sustainability policies in the Laitu Khyeng Indigenous community in Chittagong Hill Tracts (CHT), Bangladesh, and how this community wants to retake control of their land-water and build their own sustainability. Retaking control of Indigenous land-water rights and building their own sustainability demonstrates how environmental management can be used both to wipe out particular ways of knowing and lead to suffering, as in the case of state forest development on Indigenous land, or else to promote healing and a transformation of individual and community through a reconnection to history and place. Based on a very different cosmology, set of values, and ways of teaching, "retaking control of Indigenous land-water rights and building one's own sustainability" is a subtle exploration of how an Indigenous way of practice creates sustainable relationships with the land, its beings, the community, and one's own self.

Remainder of this chapter

This introductory chapter has outlined the significance and focus of this book as well as introduced the theoretical framework and methodological approaches of the research. It introduced the context of the book by describing the effects of colonialism and neocolonialism in the CHT (the Laitu Khyeng community in particular) in relation to land-water management and sustainability in the area.

Note

1 Laitu Khyeng Indigenous people are those who inhabit Gungru Muke Para and Gungru Madom Para (village) in the Bandarban District, CHT Bangladesh (Adnan, 2004; Chapola 2008).

2 Relational theoretical framework and implications for land, management, and sustainability[1]

To explore the meanings of things[2] such as land, management, and sustainability in Indigenous communities, we as researchers must first acknowledge the spirituality and experiences that connect one actor with other actors. For this reason, I suggest a relational ontology as a conceptual theoretical framework for working with Indigenous communities in relation to issues of land, management, and sustainability. This framework suggests that things are materially and spiritually connected through interactions with each other. Such a relational ontology not only challenges Western fixed meanings for actors but also makes actors responsible for their actions (Wilson, 2008). I suggest that a relational ontology can be understood as a "third space." In other words, a relational ontology can be seen as a process of deconstruction and reconstruction (Kapoor, 2008, p. 8). Things are actors in such a relational ontology; their interactions are varied, changeable, movable, and coevolving. Latour, therefore, suggests that both science and social science studies[3] need to reconfigure meanings of *things* and understandings of active actors in concepts of land, management, and sustainability (Latour, 2000).

To explain a relational ontology as my theoretical framework, in the first part of this chapter I will develop the framework with regard to various concepts such as relationality, hybridity, otherness, and scientific knowledge. In the second part, I will critically examine the concepts of management, land, and sustainability through my relational ontology. The critical discussion of the concepts of management will be twofold. First, I will explore the limitations of Western meanings of management, and second, I will explore meanings of management as forms of local culture, values, traditional experiences, spirituality, and relationships. I will then discuss how a relational ontology considers meanings of land based on everyday relational practices. Finally, I will critically discuss how the Western concept of sustainability has remained economically biased and how a relational ontology leads us to the exploration of new meanings for sustainability.

Why a relational ontology?

A relational ontology, as a theoretical framework, used through concepts of relationality, hybridity, otherness, and scientific knowledge. I suggest that a relational ontology centers on relationships and spirituality as a means of explaining not only actors but actions as well, because in a relational ontology, these cannot be explained without considering interactions with other actors.

In this section I will first explain the concept of relationality through Ingold, Deleuze, Latour, and Escobar's ideas for new ways of understanding actors and their interactions. Secondly, I will illustrate postcolonial[4] concepts of hybridity using the work of Bhabha and Whatmore and demonstrate how they may intersect with notions of a relational ontology. Finally, I will explain other possible aspects of a relational ontology through two other concepts: Said's concept of *otherness* and Lévi-Strauss's concept of *scientific knowledge*. Both of these concepts challenge our fixed ways of knowing, doing, and acting by including traditional experiences and everyday practices as significant sources of knowledge.

Relationality

A relational ontology puts relationality at its center. Actors – human and nonhuman, living and nonliving – and their actions are not only explained as relational but also as spiritually interconnected, which makes one actor responsible to the other actors (Ingold, 2011). Ingold (2011) explains that spirituality helps in understanding actors' relationships with other actors (p. 29). He thinks actors, and as such various species and organisms including humans, have *sticky* relationships. *Sticky* can be defined as multidirectional interconnectedness rather than fixed relationships. Actors and their actions cannot be fixed, limited, or attributed with any qualities. According to Ingold, an actor's actions are complex and diverse within multiple relationships.

Deleuze (2004) defines actors differently from Ingold. Although Deleuze's understanding of actors is also relational, he argues that an actor acts by the line of becoming (Deleuze & Guattari, 2004). According to Deleuze, actors follow their own lines of interaction. His actors' lines determine who the actor is and with whom they are interacting. Actors, as Deleuze explains, are not fully dependent on other actors. However, according to Ingold, an actor neither follows Deleuze's line of flight nor is an actor fixed with any accuracy. Both Ingold and Deleuze have focused on the relationships between actors to explain actors and their actions. However, their definitions still contain questions such as how an actor is inspired to interact with another. Ingold, on one hand, considers things as actors who have material and spiritual influence within their interactions. On the other hand, he does not explain much in the way of *why* actors interact with other actors. Nor has Deleuze explained how an actor can follow its own interest while interacting with other actors. However, in developing a relational ontology, both Ingold and Deleuze are helpful in explaining actors' relationships.

To overcome Ingold's and Deleuze's gaps, Latour's (2000) primary and secondary qualities can be helpful to explore actors' interactions. Primary qualities are described by Latour (2000) as physical attributes such as land, plants, species, human bodies, atoms, genes, and so on, whereas secondary qualities are identified as spirituality, relationships, feelings, smells, and interactions. To understand the actor, according to Latour, we cannot make a separation between these primary and secondary qualities. An actor's actions need to be considered as interconnected physically and spiritually. Latour's primary and secondary qualities are not two stories; rather they are complexly related. An actor's interchangeable characteristics transform things into a context in which they can be changed, moved, reflected, and ultimately become more complex. Latour (1991) shows that actors, human and nonhuman, are relational in terms of "variable geometry" (p. 116), a term he uses to explain the instability of an actor. Hence, I suggest a relational ontology neither considers actors as fixed nor rejects actors as nonactors. Like Latour, I believe a relational ontology questions not just our idea of action but also our idea of actors.

Moreover, Latour's standpoint, based on the Actor Network Theory (ANT) that he helped to develop, is that an actor cannot be understood as free and autonomous. Latour's ANT also challenges our fixed ways of knowing what counts as human and nonhuman without adding other actors, such as plants, animals, and other species, as actors. His ANT considers humans and nonhumans to be equal actors. However, Latour's (1999) extraordinary work is not unproblematic for balancing tendencies among human and nonhuman actors. In a relational ontology, actors do not maintain balance while they are interacting; rather, they are spiritually connected with each other (Whatmore, 2002).

Relationality can also be explained through Escobar's (2011) "pluriverse studies" (p. 139). His pluriverse is an open relational worldview where a single actor can be transformed into multiple actors. There is no single notion of meaning, actor, story, knowledge, civilization, or discipline. Escobar (2011) argues that "relational ontologies are those that eschew the divisions between culture, individual and community, between us and them that are central to the modern ontology" (p. 139).

Therefore, actors, including their actions and meanings, can be understood in terms of diverse and continuous relationships. Defining relationality in a relational ontology through the contributions of Deleuze, Ingold, Latour, and Escobar is not only useful for eliminating dualism between management/culture, mind/body, humans/nonhumans, and science/society but also for reconsidering things with new meanings.

Hybridity

Hybridity is another significant characteristic for exploring a relational ontology (Whatmore, 2002). A main researcher in the development of the concept of hybridity is Bhabha (2004) whose concept of hybridity challenges colonial fixity and rigidity. Here, Bhabha certainly draws upon some of Derrida's ideas to challenge narratives of fixity and rigidity that have been central to colonial conceptions of non-Western cultures. For Bhabha, hybridity takes meaning as a continuous process, which disobeys any colonial fixed authenticity. Hybridity, according to Bhabha (1985), uses a process of "the necessary deformation and displacement of all sites of discrimination and domination" (p. 154) by challenging any fixed authenticity or fixed meaning. Through the concept of hybridity,

Bhabha questions our clear sense of authenticity in distinctions and dichotomies such as management/culture, humans/nonhumans, traditional/modern, and so on (Bhabha, 2004). The clear distance between self and other becomes ambiguous. He explains, "the voice of command is interrupted by questions that arise from these heterogeneous sites and circuits of power . . . the paranoid threat from the hybrid is finally uncontainable because it breaks down the symmetry and duality of self/other, inside/outside" (2004, p. 161). Bhabha's hybridity separates neither nature and culture nor inside and outside; rather, hybridity is a way of becoming through complex relationships. Thus, Bhabha's definition of hybridity is beneficial – in a relational ontology – for understanding meanings of complex relationships as forms of becoming rather than as fixed being.

Hybridity as taken up in a relational ontology can also be explained by hybrid space, a concept articulated by well-known geographer, Whatmore (2002, 2006). Like Bhabha's ideas, Whatmore's hybrid space not only considers that actors are interconnected actors but also that they are "the condition of immanent potentiality that harbours the very possibility of their coming into being" in a fluid sense (Whatmore, 2002, p. 161). Whatmore uses hybridity to understand not only relational being but also relational *becoming* whereas her fluid sense of hybridity can be used in a relational ontology for understanding the fluidity of things. Fluidity refers to various ways of becoming. For example, land can have various identities, such as god, animal, woman, man, and so on, in its complex relationships with other actors. Thus, a hybrid sense of actors and their actions can have multiple interdependence meanings.

I suggest a relational ontology that is complex and continuous in relation to hybridity. Hybrid meanings of actors are a web of collective interactions and heterogeneous ways of becoming. Hybridity has the ability to undermine Western fixed meanings (Haluza-Delay et al., 2009). It situates things as radically antiessential (Escobar, 1999). Meanings and identities are considered effects rather than causes.

Otherness

A relational ontology also refuses hierarchical relationships among actors. According to Said (1993), otherness is a colonial idea, which positions one actor as inferior. Otherness undermines local people and their everyday practices as *less* significant. Said argues in *Culture and Imperialism* (1993) that hidden colonialist assumptions undermine local-based practices. One example is in the Jane Austen novel, *Mansfield Park*. The sugar plantation project makes local people others on their own land, creating class and gender partiality by dividing men/women, colonizers/colonized, and white/nonwhite. Instead, Said explicitly refuses to consider the actor as other and moves to a *we*, which is able to break down fundamental aspects of self and self-authenticity. He explains *othering* as a force or violence. The term *other* or *they* is not like the term *us*. *Other* suggests separation and dependency. The term *we* is relational and therefore suggests more equal opportunities. Therefore, in a relational ontology, Said's concept of *otherness* remains a significant tool for deconstructing colonial and neocolonial development and management approaches to power practices in Indigenous communities.

Scientific knowledge

Using relational ontology, traditional Indigenous land-management experiences can be considered a significant source of scientific knowledge. Such a framework sees both *science* and *traditional experiences* as valid forms of knowledge. Science, as defined by Lévi-Strauss (1998), is a new system of knowledge; similarly, he defines traditional experiences, such as mythical experiences, as forms of knowledge as well. He argues that traditional experiences, like science, can lead to future prediction. For example, if a plant is found to be poisonous, people might become cautious about using this specific plant. Through time, storytelling, and such, this observation can become a myth that functions to avoid danger in the future. Therefore, Lévi-Strauss sees that both a new scientific system of knowledge and a traditional mythical knowledge can be used to generate knowledge. He argues that if both mythical thought and scientific knowledge refuse "absolute" tendencies, they can make new possibilities (p. 19). Lévi-Strauss critiques positivist and post-positivist disciplinary truth-making for their tendency to be situated outside of societal realities. I suggest that using relational ontology in this research will, like Lévi-Strauss, reject any absolute ways of knowing.

In exploring a relational ontology as my theoretical framework, concepts of relationality, hybridity, otherness, and scientific knowledge are significant for several reasons. They lead me to understand actors as having agency in transforming impossibilities to possibilities. Actors and their actions have the power of "re-conjugating, re-contextualizing, translating the event into the politics of communities" (Mitchell, 1995, p. 114), and I understand them to be both unstable and capable of different ways of becoming.

Hence, by drawing on Ingold, Deleuze, Latour, Bhabha, Said, Lévi-Strauss, Haraway, Whatmore, and others in my investigation of meanings of management, land, and sustainability, I suggest that we need to: abandon the narrow political ideas that meanings only apply to particular human groups; confront all fixed meanings by exploring our everyday practices; and reconfigure not only the definition of actor but also the actors' actions in terms of spiritual relationships, local culture, and traditional experiences. Thus, I suggest that a relational ontology be used as the theoretical framework in this study so that meanings of land management are considered not in opposition to development and state land management nor as their complement but holistically, from multiple local relationships, and as a continuous process.

A relational ontology is respectful to "Indigenous knowing/knowledge" (Dei, 2011, p. 3) while recognizing that non-Indigenous scholars cannot access or work with Indigenous perspectives (Kovach, 2009). Using Western methodology in Indigenous research can be a challenge. Western methods have often ignored Indigenous participants' spiritual relationships and traditional experiences as sources of research knowledge (Kovach, 2009; Smith, 1999; Wilson, 2008).

Indigenous scholar Kovach (2009) raises critical views of Western methods that can undermine Indigenous knowledge by systematic coding systems. To overcome these challenges, Indigenous scholars Battiste (2000) and Wilson (2008) refer to Western research approaches that can be used for Indigenous research if researchers have empathy for their participants and aim to be accountable to Indigenous communities in their research (e.g., participatory action research (PAR), community-based research, ethnographic, autobiography, and other methods). As a non-Indigenous researcher, I prefer using a Western approach from a relational framework, which epistemologically challenges and deconstructs stereotypes, notions of unified voice, and authentic Western fixed ways of knowing (Stoecker, 2013). I am not arguing that there is only one way to interpret Indigenous relational meanings of life and relationships but rather that a Western approach from a relational theoretical perspective embraces diverse ways of knowing and takes a serious position to avoid unconscious and uncritical imposition of Western norms. Indeed, Western research approaches from a relational theoretical perspective, according to Wilson (2008), will try to understand participants' relationships "rather than treating participants only as source of research data" (p. 177).

Through a relational ontology I argue that we not only need to deconstruct our Western static vision of management but also need to move forward towards reconstructing meanings of management from people's traditional experiences. Acknowledging Escobar (2010, 2008), Latour (2004, 2000), and others, I also support management as a static concept that requires critical understanding. In exploring meanings of management in Indigenous communities, we need to gather the knowledge of traditional experiences beyond disciplinary boundaries and other ideas that narrow our vision. I suggest that a relational ontology, therefore, will consider multiple realities, relationships, and interactions based on our traditional knowledge. It refers us to an alternative ontology which leads us from the colonial fixed concept of management to a relational concept of management (Escobar, 2011, 1996, 1999; Ingold, 2011).

Implications in land, management, and sustainability

It is important to critically discuss how a relational ontology can be used to explore the concepts of management, land, and sustainability in Indigenous communities. Therefore, I will discuss the concepts of management as forms of local culture, values, traditional experiences, spirituality, and relationships. I will then review how a relational ontology considers meanings of land based on everyday relational practices. Finally, I will critically examine how the concept of sustainability has remained economically biased and how a relational ontology leads us to consider new meanings of sustainability.

Land

I propose a relational ontology understanding of land as being connected with people's everyday practices and as a hybrid space which involves multiple relational practices. In exploring meanings of land, Ingold's (2011) concepts of *life* and *room* are helpful. He explains that *life* is lived and open instead of structured and fixed. On the other hand, *room* "affords scope for growth and movements" (p. 147). Land as a form of room does not have modern boundaries; it does not have walls but only vast ground, and it does not have roofs but only open sky. Ingold (2011) thinks, "the idea that places are situated in space is the *product* of this inversion, and is not given prior to it" (p. 147). Ingold considers land in our everyday practices as open space where things become actors. Land is not fixed; land is an actor, which is able to influence our actions but also our ways of becoming. Therefore, the meaning of land can be understood, according to a relational ontology, as the movement of relationships.

Land as an object, in a relational ontology, is not important; rather, what is important is its relationship with other actors. Land engages humans and nonhumans in ways that show how actors are spiritually connected with one another. Considering a relational ontology, Wainwright and Barnes (2009) argue that land is a transfixing and dynamic spatial flow of interactions. Thus, in understanding meanings of land, relationships are fundamental. Once humans and nonhumans are connected with land in their everyday relational practices, meanings are coconstituted as a totality. Land becomes relationships, culture, and spirituality where humans and nonhumans connect in their everyday interactions. Wainwright and Barnes' (2009) understanding of land is highly reflected in the multiple Indigenous meanings of land, where implications of land are considered holistically, dynamically, relationally, and continuously (Nelson, 2006), being connected to people, animals, trees, plants, dreams, and spirituality.

Land is a symbol of respect in many Indigenous communities, which strongly differs from the Western fixed sense. For example, Bloch (2008), a non-Indigenous scholar studying within Indigenous communities, argues that Indigenous people are emotionally and spiritually connected with their places, forests, and houses. He shows that in the *Zafimaniry* community in eastern Madagascar, land, just like the sun and the sky, is seen as a *god* who takes care of them. Bloch shows that the relationship between people and the land and gods is respectful, which makes humans responsible actors. Further, the meaning of house is not only a place to live but also a symbol of respecting, blessing, and connecting with ancestors. A house's different parts have different meanings. For example, the hardest wood is associated with a man's marriage, and a cooking pot or a large wooden spoon is associated with women's marriage. A single house transforms to a holy house and center of the village. The *Zafimaniry* community's reproductive success and social success are attached to their land as well, whereas *Zafimaniry* strength, political power, and different ways of being may not be explainable without explaining their relationships with land. In a similar contemporary example from the *Kissa* Indigenous community from the Republic of Guinea, Fairhead and Leach (1997) show that the *Kissa* community's everyday practices, their identity, political relationships, women's fertility, and the political ecology of the forest are connected with their traditional experiences and relationships with trees. There is no way to ignore the language of trees in their forest management. Their traditional experiences with trees and forest lead them to interact with or manage their forest and their everyday life. Hence, meanings of land are not limited by fixed boundaries in many indigenous communities.

Management

I propose that a relational theoretical framework critically examines the general colonial concept of management. Studies (Lertzman, 2010; Lertzman & Vredenburg, 2005) have found the Western and Indigenous meanings of *management* carry fundamentally different meanings stemming from different worldviews with differentiated philosophies, practices, and methods. Dudgeon and Berkes (2003) suggest that the Western and Indigenous understanding of management in many Indigenous communities are ontologically contradictory owing to differing worldviews, practices, and methods. Therefore, to explore meanings of management in relation to a relational ontology, this section will first critically examine Western fixed meanings of management and, second, explore meanings of management from the perspective of local culture, which moves beyond Western fixed meanings.

The Western and Indigenous meanings of management fundamentally carry different meanings in terms of different worldviews with their own philosophy, practices, and methods (Lertzman, 2010; Lertzman & Vredenburg, 2005). Dudgeon and Berkes (2003) suggest that the Western and Indigenous understanding of management in many Indigenous communities are ontologically contradicted with different worldviews, practices, and methods. The very idea of Western understanding/knowledge of management is a technique to be not only incorporated but also oppressed into Indigenous understanding/knowledge of management (Nadasdy, 1999). The concept of management has not changed from colonial perspectives in the neocolonial era, leaving numerous unjust forest-development projects unchallenged in many parts of the world (Nadasdy, 2011, 2003; Escobar, 2008, 1995). If Western management does not honor and/or consider Indigenous perspectives as significant, it can lead to economic inequality, displacement, loss of traditional lifestyles, and significant environmental damage to the many Indigenous communities (Nadasdy, 2003).

The Western understanding/knowledge of management tends to focus on technique; this idea of management not only subsumes Indigenous knowledge of management, in many regions it also considers Indigenous knowledge as illegitimate (Nadasdy, 2003). Escobar (1995) explains Western management knowledge "relied exclusively on one knowledge system, namely the modern Western one. The dominance of this knowledge system has dictated the marginalization and disqualification of no Western knowledge systems" (p. 13). Nadasdy (2003) states that Western meanings of management take "for granted existing power relations between aboriginal people and the state by assuming that Indigenous knowledge is simply a new form of 'data' to be incorporated into already existing management bureaucracies" (p. 15). First Nations scholars Battiste and Henderson (2000) take this further, arguing that attempts to define environmental management systems are inherently colonial, based on a Eurocentric need to categorize and control.

The concept of management has not changed from colonial perspectives in the neocolonial era, leaving numerous unjust forest-development projects in many parts of the world unchallenged. Gomes (2004) gives an example from the *Semai* Indigenous community in Malaysia (known as *Orang Asli*) to show how the state has largely used a fixed scientific concept of management to control the *Semai*'s local resources. The government's management tools, envisioning development as the only way forward, became fixed, ignoring *Semai* Indigenous traditional practices as "backward," "traditional," or useless (Gomes, 2004, p. 2). To enhance *development*, Indigenous people have been forced to use new modern technology over their traditional practices; Gomes argues that the technological development project was mainly for state and outsider profit. The management model has not only undermined local land relationships but has also led to land alienation and identity crisis in the *Semai* Indigenous community. Therefore, meanings of management in the *Semai* Indigenous community have not only remained artificial but they have also become exploitative. Hence, I refuse to use my relational ontology to consider management as something fixed or with a single meaning (Law, 2004).

Western management processes create a subaltern group. For instance, studies (Berkes, 1999; Fletcher, 2008; Lertzman, 2010) show that with Western forms of management processes, local people become subaltern in their own land. We use the term *subaltern*, according to Young (2003), to refer a member of the lower classes and social groups who are at the margin of society. According to Young, subaltern refers to a person without human agency. Within Western state management processes, local people become socially, politically, and geographically outside the hegemonic power structure of the colony and colonial homeland (Spivak, 2006). Therefore, South Asian Indigenous scholars Chakma (2010) and Roy's (2000) studies on Bangladeshi Indigenous communities show how Bangladeshi management agencies (government, multinational corporations, and NGOs) justify state management projects over Indigenous people by saying that these people (subalterns) are ignorant and they do not know what to do or how to change for the better.

In contrast, Indigenous knowledge in terms of environmental management extends from a community-based and decentralized prioritization of resource management (Bunnell, 2008; Butt & McMillan, 2009). For example, Article 8 of the Convention on Biological Diversity explains Indigenous environmental management as "respect, preserve and maintain knowledge, innovations and practices of indigenous and local communities embodying traditional lifestyles relevant for the conservation and sustainable use of biological diversity" (United Nations, 2013). On this point, Berkes (2003) explains that Indigenous environmental management knowledge has been rediscovered as a model for a recognition of their land rights, identity, interests, and a healthy interaction with and use of the environment to gain new perspectives about the relationship between humans and management. Dudgeon and Berkes (2003) explain that Indigenous ways of understanding management are oriented according to Indigenous traditional ways of knowing, practicing, and informing cultivation culture on their land. Indigenous scholars Battiste and Henderson (2000) see Indigenous management as a mode or component order; its great diversity is a reflection of ecological diversity.

Indigenous ways of understanding management can be explained according to Indigenous traditional ways of knowing, practicing, and informing cultivation culture in their land (Dudgeon & Berkes, 2003). Indigenous meanings of management promote local people and local knowledge. Indigenous knowledge in natural resource management is given less attention by the state government and nongovernmental agencies in many Indigenous communities (Lertzman, 2010; Bohensky & Maru, 2011). For instance, Canadian Indigenous scholar Marie Battiste states that Indigenous knowledge is situated within and from local practice and is "the expression of the vibrant relationships between the people, their ecosystems, and the other living beings and spirits that share their land" (2000, p. 42). She also argues that "All aspects of this knowledge are interrelated and cannot be separated from the traditional territories of the people concerned" (p. 42). Nadasdy (1999) explains that if Western environmental management is not connected with local knowledge, it can be challenging for the local communities. Escobar (1995) explains that Western management knowledge, which is outside of local communities, "Relied exclusively on one knowledge system, namely the modern Western one. The dominance of this knowledge system has dictated the marginalization and disqualification of no Western knowledge systems" (p. 13).

Thus, I suggest a relational ontology that will consider meanings of management as part of everyday culture. Parkin (1997) shows that in the West Bengal, India, Hindu community the tree is a powerful actor in understanding human lifestyles. The tree has the power to change a person's social status, their identity, and their relationships. For the community Parkin is studying, the meanings of the trees are complex relationships, which can play significant roles in everyday practice. Trees are not only objects or symbolic metaphors but also material actors who have the ability to interact in everyday practices. For example, the notion of a *marrying tree* can break down the Western sense of the nature-culture dichotomy. Men and women in the West Bengal, India, Hindu community, for instance, cannot get married to a person without marrying other actors. Marriage with actors such as trees, tokens, pots, the sun, rocks, a mountain, and so on not only shows a new sense of actors but also shows different implications for actors. Interacting with or marrying is meant to increase fertility among humans, plants, animals, fish, and so on. Therefore, Parkin (1997) explains, "not only people but also the gods, the sun, and the moon – and even fishing nets and hunting weapons – are ritually 'married,' otherwise they will be of no use" (p. 55). Marriage, he argues, is not only a social status or a fertility ritual leading to childbirth but is also a process of reconnecting with land. *Actors*, such as trees, land, and rocks, live, have souls and are active aspects of everyday life. Similarly, non-Indigenous scholar Brightman (1993), who studies the *Cree* Indigenous community in Canada, shows that spirituality plays a significant role in understanding the interaction of Indigenous people. Brightman shows a semiotic relationship between *Cree* people, arguing that "Crees conceive themselves simultaneously as hunters of animals and as the prey of monsters who are the hunter of humans" (p. 136). A dreamer uses magical power to kill *witikos* – those who do not care for others. Through spiritual relationships with animals, *Cree* people become responsible, powerful, and self-sufficient. Spiritual relationships with animals not only protect *Cree* from food crises but also save the animals in their territory. Thus, management has diverse meanings in a relational ontology.

Through a relational ontology, I argue that we not only need to deconstruct our static Western vision of management but we also need to move forward toward reconstructing meanings of management from people's experiences. Acknowledging Escobar (2008, 2010, 2008), Latour (2000, 2004), and others, I support management as a dynamic concept that requires critical understanding. In exploring meanings of management in Indigenous communities, we need to gather the knowledge of spiritual and relational experiences beyond Western disciplinary boundaries and other ideas that narrow our vision. I suggest that a relational ontology, therefore, will consider multiple realities, relationships, and interactions based on traditional knowledge, leading us from a colonial fixed concept of management to a relational concept of management (Escobar, 1996, 1999, 2011; Ingold, 2011).

Sustainability

A relational ontology can be used to question fixed meanings of management policies and, instead, define management in terms of sustainability. It can challenge not only management development projects' fundamental goals (e.g., economic growth) and outcomes (e.g., othering) but also any fixed authority over local people's spiritual and relational practices. Relational ontology stresses meanings of sustainability as situated in practice and critiques antidevelopmental stances that consider relational practice as the center.

I suggest through a relational ontology that traditional experiences and spiritual relationships have significant influence on meanings of sustainability in Indigenous communities. Therefore, meanings of sustainability in a relational ontology move beyond the dualism of science or social science. Meanings are processes of understanding the "value of traditional and neo-traditional or otherwise local resource management" (Folke et al., 1998, p. 43). Considering traditional experiences and spiritual relationships as significant sources of knowledge in exploring sustainability not only makes us responsible for our actions but also creates critical space for *reimagination*, for others to consider these actors as relational. Hence, Payne (2009) argues sustainability is "being for others, rather than being for self" (p. 318).

Sustainability not only connects humans and environments, it also creates many possibilities in rethinking practices. Escobar (1999) argues that "sustainability cannot be defined independently of the specific ecological, cultural, technological, and economic conditions of the appropriation of management," rather, sustainability stands as holistic (p. 26). Similarly, Agyeman et al. (2003) explain sustainability as "just sustainability" (p. 324). These views challenge dominant management-development paradigms, which have a strong tendency to favor development, to ignore others, and to disassociate human and place relationships. Likewise, Davison (2008) argues that sustainability is an interaction between normative claims and practical concerns in creative change and open-ended dialogue. Sustainability, as hybrid spaces that are lived within (what Whatmore (2006) calls *livingness*), models the connection between all bodies. *Livingness* redirects material concerns: "thing-ness of things' – bodies, objects, arrangements" – are always in-the-making and "humans are always in composition with non humanity, never outside of a sticky web of connections or ecology" (p. 603). New meanings of sustainability create different alternatives of practice when they suggest that all things have agency, and this is associated with practice. Sustainability as livingness or practices shifts our thinking from cultural geography's self-consciousness phenomena "I think, therefore I am" to one of "I think, therefore I act" (Whatmore, 2006, p. 603). Livingness or practice-based understandings relocate social agency in various ways. Meanings of sustainability in a relational ontology can be defined as following:

> a cumulative body of knowledge, practice, and belief, evolving by adaptive processes and handed down through generations by cultural transmission, about the relationship of living beings (including humans) with one another and with their environment.
>
> (Berkes, 1999, p. 8)

Therefore, sustainability can be understood for exploring land-management as offering a "different way of imagining life" (Escobar, 2011, p. 139). Sustainability is respectful of relationships, expectations, daydreams, and spirituality, which enable us to imagine (Escobar, 2010; McKenzie et al., 2009). Drawing on collective diverse understandings, I suggest sustainability is an ongoing process that is linked to our imagination, dreams, and spirituality. Understanding meanings and implications of sustainability as a practice-based, complex, critical, and ongoing process can not only engage us in a complex conversation of sustainability but also create space for our dreams, imagination, and spirituality to enter into our everyday eco-practice.

In sum, I suggest a relational ontology that implicitly leaves behind all prioritizations that are involved in modern dualistic thinking. Meanings of *actors* in this framework neither work with predetermined relations nor should they involve hierarchy. Rather, in using relational ontology as my conceptual framework, I suggest meanings of actors – such as in conceptions of land, management, and sustainability – as hybrid processes, which are continuously shifting, changing, moving, transforming, assembling, and becoming more complex. Such a relational ontology calls on our everyday, practice-based understandings to deconstruct our preexisting ideas of land, management, and sustainability. This reconfiguring of the meanings of actors and their material agency will be an ongoing process, one that critically examines power relations, uneven history, and globalization.

Relational understandings of land and sustainability refuse management as a fixed concept. I have developed a relational ontology for local people's everyday

34 Relational theoretical framework

practices where meanings of land, management, and sustainability are considered relational, part of the social order, and connected to traditional experiences, one's own body, dreams, and spirituality.

In this chapter, I explained a relational ontology as one that not only deconstructs our fixed vision regarding actors and actors' actions but also moves us toward a better understanding of our complex interactions. Such a relational ontology prepares us to understand multiple realities, relationships, and spirituality based on our everyday practices.

Notes

1 Some parts of this chapter were previously published in the *Local Environment: The International Journal of Justice and Sustainability* (Datta, 2015). Reprint permission received.
2 I use the term *things* to mean both human and nonhuman actors, such as humans, animals, land, sky, moon, rocks, different species, traditional experiences, spiritual relationships, and so on (Aikenhead & Ogawa, 2007). *Things* are actors; they have material agency that can influence other actors' actions (Escobar, 2011; Latour, 2000).
3 *Science* and *social science* are terms I use to define areas of disciplinary study that become problematic not because of their scientific tendencies but for their unequal structuring and separating tendencies from each other (Haraway, 2004; Latour, 2000).
4 *Postcolonial* subjects are codified discursively to create meaning for everyday living. Postcolonial theory provides a pathway toward exploring multiplicities (Gandhi, 1998).

3 Participatory action research and researcher responsibilities[1]

This chapter explores the relational participatory action research (PAR) frameworks that have been developed to allow non-Indigenous researchers, along with Indigenous coresearcher participants, to learn and honor Indigenous stories. Specifically, in the context of PAR research in the Chittagong Hill Tracts (CHT) of Bangladesh, we[2] outline: (a) potential challenges between Indigenous research paradigms and Western research paradigms, (b) the situation of the non-Indigenous researcher in relation to the Indigenous community, (c) challenges associated with the non-Indigenous researcher's selection of a research site, (d) collaboration throughout the research process, and (e) the processes of developing and maintaining responsibilities. The aim is not to offer simple answers to such challenges but to highlight the manner in which such processes can be addressed. This chapter may provide practical insight for future non-Indigenous researchers working with Indigenous communities through a participatory sharing process with Indigenous coresearcher participants, Elders, leaders, Knowledge-holders, and youth.

Research methodology greatly influences both the research process and its outcomes. To explore and situate the researcher in research, it is important to discuss the researcher's position and methodology (Battiste, 2008; Dei, 1999; Smith, 2008; Wilson, 2008, 2007). Through our[3] research in Bangladesh[4] we learned that we needed to attend to a number of responsibilities in doing participatory action research (PAR) with Indigenous communities. Such responsibilities included situating the researcher within the participants' community (i.e., building trustful relationships), empowering participants, recognizing spiritual and relational knowledge, and taking a political stand for the participants' community (Battiste, 2008; Smith, 2008; Wilson, 2008, 2007). In this chapter we discuss our research journey as follows: first, we explain our decision to choose PAR as our research methodology, including how it complemented a relational research framework; second, we discuss our responsibilities in PAR and its benefits to the participants' community; third, we explain the process we went through in selecting a research site in Bangladesh, collecting the research data, and analyzing the collected data; and, finally, we discuss how the PAR method was helpful in reclaiming the indigenous voice.

Participatory action research (PAR) methodological framing

Participatory action research (PAR) as a relational ontology is respectful to "Indigenous knowing/knowledge" (Datta et al., 2014; Dei, 2011, p. 3), while recognizing that non-Indigenous scholars cannot access or work with indigenous perspectives (Kovach, 2009). Using PAR, a Western methodology, in Indigenous research can be a challenge. Western methods have often ignored Indigenous participants' spiritual relationships and traditional experiences as sources of research To order to overcome these challenges, Indigenous scholars Battiste (2000) and Wilson (2008) refer to PAR as an approach that can be used for Indigenous research if researchers have empathy for their participants and aim to be accountable to Indigenous communities in their research. As a non-Indigenous researcher, I used the PAR approach from a relational framework, which epistemologically challenges and deconstructs stereotypes, notions of unified voice, and authentic Western fixed ways of knowing (Stoecker, 2013). I am not arguing that there is only one way to interpret Indigenous relational meanings of life and relationships, but rather that a PAR approach embraces diverse ways of knowing and takes a serious position to avoid unconscious and uncritical imposition of Western authentic otherness. Indeed, PAR in this research, according to Wilson (2008), tried to understand participants' relationships "rather than treating participants only as source of research data" (p. 177).

The researcher's main accountability in a PAR methodology is to honor participants' spiritual relationships and holistic worldviews as well demonstrating reciprocity (Wilson & Pence, 2010). The researcher's responsibility is to be actively engaged in giving voice to marginalized, silenced, and ignored communities. Similarly, Ferreira and Gendron (2011) argue that when conducting research with Indigenous communities, the researcher needs to consider each participant's knowledge respectfully and as significant; in fact, researchers using PAR may want to consider each participant as a "coresearcher and co-learner" (p. 157). Researcher's accountabilities open possibilities for participant needs (Creswell, 2007). Thus, positioning the researcher in relation to the research is vital for PAR (Wilson, 2008).

Situating myself as researcher

In exploring the questions set out in this thesis, I must clearly acknowledge my socialization, identity, education, and professional experiences to understand my participatory action research (PAR) ontology and epistemology in relation to my relational theoretical framework. Scholars such as Becker (1967), Ferreira and Gendron (2011), Meyer (2001), McCarthey and Moje (2002), and Smith (1999) argue that a researcher's responsibilities are to conduct significant research rather than to acknowledge their personal identity. Indigenous scholar Dei (1999) argues that

> Locating oneself is important to knowledge production and validation. It is also crucial for how a text/discourse is read, understood, and interpreted. Personal location contributes to the production of meanings.
>
> (p. 397)

Although I agree that researchers should conduct meaningful work, they should also acknowledge that who they are will affect the processes and outcomes of their research. Similarly to Mead (1934), I think a person's mind, self, and society construct relations and acts relationally. Mead goes on to argue that people act and think according to their socialization. Therefore, Torre and Ayala (2009) argue, it is the researcher's responsibility to make space to rethink their identity and challenge ways of being. Asking "Who am I as a researcher?" is an important issue when conducting research within Indigenous communities (Smith, 1999; Wilson, 2008). I agree with Wilson (2007) who suggests that research knowledge cannot be separated from who we are as researchers and what we are doing. Research is about exploring relationships "with our environment, families, ancestors, ideas and the cosmos around us [which] shape who we are and how we will conduct our research" (p. 194). Therefore, a researcher's identity is important to their research.

My cross-cultural identity, such as my socialization, relationships, education, and professional experiences, is important in discussing who I am as a researcher. I was born into and grew up in a minority[5] family. Minority communities have many difficulties in decision-making processes in my nation-state, a nation-state that is deeply associated with a particular Islamic religion (Mohsin, 2002). Minorities, including Indigenous communities, have been regarded as an underclass (Adnan, 2004; Mohsin, 2002). Like Indigenous communities, my community people are well acquainted with the meaning of oppression, mainstream negligence, and economic hardship from the mainstream nation-state and mainstream community. Being part of a minority community, I have seen how my family struggled in its everyday life for production and cultivation, land rights, and education (Human Right Congress for Bangladesh Minorities Report, 2013; Iva, 2010). Several questions remain for me: "Why have we been displaced from our motherland?" "Why do we not have land rights in our ancestral land?" Our minority identity has made our lives, like those of Indigenous communities, vulnerable in our own land (Internal Displace Monitoring Centre Report, 2015). As minority citizens, we always feel that our lives are not our own. My experiences have led me to do this research to find a space for reclaiming Indigenous and minority land-water rights in many parts of Bangladesh. In fact, in terms of everyday oppression, as part of a minority who has been displaced from its original land by the mainstream, my community and many Indigenous communities are not so different. Therefore, this research is a part of our collective struggle and a political stand.

Like those who are a part of an Indigenous community, my socialization was also different from the mainstream community. I was a male person in a nation that favors a patriarchal system; however, I grew up in a maternal family structure. This is important to me because the male-biased nation-state does not recognize a maternal family structure. Women are excluded and considered second-class citizens in many decision-making processes. As the head of a family, a woman has to face many difficulties in her everyday life (Kabeer, 2011). Because my father passed away just after I was born, my mother and sisters assumed the role of decision-makers, as in many Indigenous communities around the world. My upbringing has enhanced my understanding of different socialization processes, such as those common in Indigenous communities in the Chittagong Hill Tracts (CHT).

I refer to my identity as cross-cultural because of my interdisciplinary education and experiences. My first university degree was in sociology at Shahjalal University of Science and Technology in Bangladesh. My master's was in criminal justice from Monmouth University in the United States. Recently, I completed my PhD from the School of Environmental Sustainability at the University of Saskatchewan, Canada. During my studies I have completed several courses and done research work in various disciplines, such as foundational education, anthropology, environment and sustainability, sociology, mathematics, criminal justice, statistics, computer science, social work, and economics. My education has taken me back and forth between a variety of disciplinary understandings, offering me opportunities to explore meanings of land entitlement, women's empowerment in Bangladesh minority communities, and Bangladeshi immigrants' knowledge of justice in the United States. My interdisciplinary education made me well aware of my responsibilities as a researcher. In addition, my professional research work with Indigenous communities helped me to build relationships with various Indigenous communities.

In my university life, I have actively participated in various minority rights, Indigenous land rights, Indigenous women's rights, and Indigenous language movements. I had numerous opportunities to meet and discuss their land rights, displacement, and violence with CHT Indigenous leaders. As a research professional, I have also had opportunities to work with various Indigenous communities in Australia, Canada, Finland, India, New Zealand, Norway, and the United States. Through my graduate studies and community works, I have gained practical research skills on building trust, honoring and respecting participants' knowledge, and undertaking literature reviews, interviews, participant observation, content analysis, and examining researcher's accountability in the research process.

In addition to my teaching and research experience, I have nearly fifteen years of professional work experience with Indigenous communities after and prior to beginning my PhD. Working in Bangladesh as a research associate, I gained extensive professional experience in the fields of community-based research, social inequality, developmental politics and globalization, and social justice advocacy. Having been involved with minority and Indigenous youth groups and people in the Chittagong Hill Tracts (CHT) through this work, I participated in various research studies on Indigenous land rights, women's rights, and environmental rights movements, with numerous opportunities to meet and coordinate meetings with various government/nongovernment stakeholders and CHT Indigenous leaders.

Centering participants' voices in Western research is a challenge. Although I have been engaged in participatory community-based research, I have also learned how to bring out a community's voice. For instance, I have served for more than three years on various university administrative committees, as vice president academic of the University of Saskatchewan Graduate Student Association (2014–2015); the University's Sustainability Committee (2013–2015), the search committee for Vice-Provost Teaching and Learning (2012), and the University of Saskatchewan Graduate Student Transit Committee (2013). This formal training helped me how to bring collective voice in a formal discussion.

My involvements in community activities beyond the university helped me to understand who I am a researcher. Through my last fifteen years of community activities I learned that as researcher, I should think, act, and response my responsibilities as part of the community. Participants should be also part of the researcher's needs. Research should benefit both participants and researcher. My active participation in various social and justice movements, (such as the Idle No More Movement, Black rights movements, Standing Rock movement, First Nation's Land Rights) helped me understand my responsibilities and accountabilities as a researcher and community member. I expect to continue with community activities for the rest of my life because I am by necessity a vehement critic of injustice.

In sum, my cross-cultural identity through my socialization, education, and professional experiences has made me well aware of my own position and responsibilities toward my participants' communities. I have learned that my identity is important in this world because it provides an alternative. As a non-Indigenous researcher, my empathy, learning, and professional experiences help me learn how to be respectful toward participants, particularly Indigenous participants with whom I have connected over the last couple of years. My unique cross-cultural background is well suited to understanding a relational paradigm's ontology, epistemology, and methodology, which is informed by Indigenous paradigms (Smith, 2008; Tuck, 2012; Wilson, 2008).

Research design

Participatory selecting of a research site story

The field site I chose for my research was a Laitu Khyeng Indigenous community in Chittagong Hill Tracts (CHT), Bangladesh. Getting access to this site was difficult because the Canadian Foreign Affairs Ministry had issued a travel advisory. Therefore, accessing the field site for my research was an unexpected challenge.

Due to the travel advisory, I had initially hoped to use the alternate back-up sites outlined in my proposal. However, during my first two weeks in Bangladesh attempting to visit these sites (one of which was my hometown), it became clear that it was not safe for me to stay and do research in them. Current political unrest associated with an upcoming election and other factors had made the whole country quite unstable. Unsure how to proceed, I made contact through a phone conversation with one of the Laitu Khyeng Indigenous leaders regarding my proposed research proposal and the possibility of using their home community as a field site for my research. Four of the Laitu Khyeng Indigenous leaders and one of the Elders from the Laitu Khyeng community came to my hometown after two days of travel to request in person that I do my research with them. I was told by the Laitu Khyeng Elder and leaders that the CHT area where the community was located was relatively safe compared to my hometown and other centers of extremist movements within Bangladesh. Ironically, due to recent unrest across the country, the CHT was a safer place for me as a minority in Bangladesh as opposed to many of the urban centers for which there was no travel advisory issued. Through some research, I found I could stay in a community that had been unaffected by the violence near the CHT if I was unable to visit their villages due to the travel advisory from the Canadian Ministry of Foreign Affairs.

The Laitu Khyeng people I was in communication with wanted the research to be conducted because none had been conducted with the community in the past. Because the community did not have any opportunities to reach the national government's land-forest policy-makers to inform them of the community's needs, they wished to pursue expressing their needs through the research project. These needs included their need to protect their motherland. Though I told them that my research could not change their situation, I was told by the Elder within the community I had contacted that they understood this but that they wanted to proceed with the research anyway. They wanted to conduct the research with me and to collaborate on an analysis of it.

Because I had preexisting relationships and contact with Khyeng Indigenous Elders and leaders, and given that the CHT was safe for me, especially in contrast with other areas of Bangladesh, I decided to attempt to continue with my planned research. For this process, I completed a travel exemption application to enter the CHT with the University of Saskatchewan, all the while having limited access to electric power and internet access. This was an extended process due to reviews by the committee, School of Environment and Sustainability (SENS), the International Student and Study Abroad Centre, the Risk Management Office, and the Provost's Office. While awaiting processing of the travel advisory, I was unable to visit the Khyeng community; however, another community outside of the CHT, the Dolbonia Para, was close enough to enable me to stay there while communicating with the research site.

To start the research process, four coresearcher participants were recruited from the Khyeng community located within the CHT by the Khyeng Indigenous Elders and leaders. These coresearcher participants gathered data within the Khyeng villages originally planned as research sites over a period of four months while meeting with me outside the CHT each night to go over data collection and analysis. Due to the travel restriction on the area housing the Khyeng community, my research became funding-oriented to compensate the coresearcher participants and to cover my accommodation. Funding was used to pay for participants' transportation and food as they traveled to visit me in the adjacent community. Luckily, the University of Saskatchewan's Dr. Rui Feng Research Award and the International Development Research Centre (IDRC) Doctoral Research Award were helpful in covering these expenditures. Coordinating travel time with participants was a challenge for a number of reasons. For example, the Bangladesh Islamic extremist movement triggered countrywide transportation strikes limiting bus and train mobility, which led to a transportation crisis at several points during my stay. The rainy weather was another impediment to dependable travel. However, participants and I solved these issues through sharing processes in our regular sharing circles and group meetings.

Though I was in a safe place that was both away from the violence and political unrest in much of Bangladesh while still honoring the travel advisory, I had to reconcile one additional issue with the University of Saskatchewan to conduct my research. The university took four months to process my travel exemption application and did not give me permission to visit the actual Laitu Khyeng Indigenous community within the CHT I was studying until I returned to Saskatoon, Canada. This was despite the fact that the political situation in Bangladesh had changed drastically since the travel advisory had been issued about the CHT region. During my time in Bangladesh, I was continuously informed that I was at greater risk in areas *outside* of the CHT, and that, as a minority citizen within Bangladesh, the research site of the Khyeng community I was researching was a *safer* place for me. In retrospect, this has been an education for me in noting that the context of foreign travel advisories can change swiftly and may not always be appropriate for a researcher doing fieldwork in a rapidly changing political situation. Despite the Bangladesh political situation and long delays in the university's processing of my travel exemption, I was able to successfully complete my four months of fieldwork and share my research results with the community according to my original proposal.

Participatory participants' selection processes

Participants in the study included coresearcher participants, Elders, Knowledge-holders, leaders, and youth (people between fifteen and thirty years of age are referred to as youth, according to the Elders).

To select participants for this study, I recruited four coresearcher participants from the Khyeng community located within the CHT who were chosen by the Khyeng Indigenous Elders and leaders. Because I had previous personal and working relationships with Laitu Khyeng Elders, Knowledge-holders, and leaders, I asked them to help me to recruit coresearcher participants. In my coresearcher recruiting letter I clearly mentioned the purpose of the study (through discussing with community Elders, Knowledge-holders, and leaders) and their (i.e., coresearcher participants) responsibilities to investigate the traditional and current forms of land management.

The four coresearcher participants' involvement with this research was vital. They continuously engaged and participated through all the field research and data analysis processes, such as helping to identify volunteer participants (such as Elders, Knowledge-holders, and youth participants); facilitating traditional sharing circles with Elders, Knowledge-holders, and youth participants; conducting participant observation and photovoice; recording traditional sharing circles and individual storytelling discussions; maintaining a commonplace book to record personal observations, art, poems, experiences, stories with the environment, field notes; helping to code and analyse research data, and so on.

Elders, Knowledge-holders, and leaders

Because I knew the Laitu Indigenous community, it was not difficult to identify potential Elders, Knowledge-holders, and leader participants for this research;

however, Elders and leaders guided the coresearcher participants and me. They provided potential participant information and how to contact them. I shared and discussed our research questions, objectives, and research methods for building participatory research processes (Datta et al., 2015). Due to oral versus print-based literacy, they gave their consent verbally – in other words, I read the consent form to them and the coresearcher participants signed it for them after they (Elders, Knowledge-holders, and leaders) gave oral consent. I gave a copy of the form to each participant for their records.

Youths

Elders and coresearcher participants helped me to find youth participants. The age range was fifteen to twenty-eight from various gender backgrounds. Coresearcher participants and I explained and discussed our research objectives and benefits. We also discussed their activities in this research, particularly photovoice. We told them that we wanted to learn their views on the places they identify with the cultural knowledge and practices of this area. As per the study's focus on participatory research methodology, we also needed youth to work specifically with me on the data-collecting process. Hence, of the eight youth, five (three female and two male) volunteered to join us during traditional sharing circles (conversations with Elders, Knowledge-holders, and leaders) and other aspects of the research process. The youths' guardians gave their oral consent (coresearcher participants signed a consent form) on behalf of the youth (those who were under eighteen).

The process of selecting participants and getting their consent took close to two weeks. This was necessary because I had to give the participants time, learn the cultural practices of the community, and build relationships and trust with participants.

Participatory data-collection stories

A number of the data-collection methods I employed were aligned with participatory action research (PAR) methodology in engaging community participation, respecting local knowledge, and increasing participant benefits (as outlined in my research proposal). Research methods used within the research included: traditional sharing circles, individual storytelling, commonplace books, participant observation, and photovoice. These methods were undertaken according to the participants' culture, traditional experiences, and spirituality. All data collection was carried out in Bengali because my participants' everyday communicative language was Bengali and Khyeng, in both the Gungru Mukh Para and Gunru Modrom Para Khyeng communities. Khyeng language was not used because I could not speak Khyeng. Sharing circles and individual storytelling processes were conducted on a collective and individual basis.

The interviews were audio-recorded and transcribed, then safely locked away in a secure location on the research site. Two copies of data were kept. One copy was saved with a Khyeng Indigenous Elder, and a second copy was saved with the supervising researcher. There were not any foreseeable risks in terms of privacy and confidentiality because there was no public access to the raw data except by the Khyeng Indigenous participants. Participants' (e.g., coresearcher participants and participants) identity was well documented so that their voices could be heard because all participants wanted this to be the case (as indicated in the consent forms).

Traditional sharing circles (TSC)

Traditional sharing circle (TSC) is one of the most important research methods for conducting research with Indigenous communities (Lovell, 2007; Simpson, 2014). TSC refers here to focus group discussion (FGD) following local cultural norms and format (Lovell, 2007). TSC used in this research was in accordance with the Khyeng community's cultural practice. The main points to be explored included existing land-management practices, traditional experiences (and their exceptions), and what we referred to as sustainability for future land management. There were five Elders, three leaders, three Knowledge-holders, and five youth participant names proposed for TSC by community Elders.

The TSC method was both a learning and a sharing process for me. Throughout the process I learned many Laitu Khyeng stories as well as shared many of my own stories with the participants. We carried out three TSCs during my four months of fieldwork, all organized outside of CHT in the adjacent community I was staying in. The first two TSCs were conducted during the first and second month of my field research. Both of these were two hours long and arranged during weekends so that participants did not have to contend with any of the road strikes. These two TSCs were followed by lunch because participants had traveled a long way from their villages. However, the third and final TSC was four hours long and was followed by overnight accommodation for the participants as well as dinner.

Individual story sharing (ISS)

ISS played a significant role in our PAR research because it helped to explore individual's spiritual and relational stories, memories, personal experiences, and expectations (Datta et al., 2015; Kovach, 2010). ISS was conducted in a similar fashion as traditional sharing circles (i.e., drawing on sharing stories from the diverse set of participants, participants' accommodation being provided and time being compensated, and sharing processes following a similar narrative) but in a dialogue between two individual as opposed to group sharing circles. There were nine ISS sessions conducted during my four months in the field, including a diverse group of participants, such as Elders, Knowledge-holders, leaders, and youth participants. Each meeting was forty to sixty minutes in length. ISS were recorded, and, at a later time, transcribed by myself and the coresearchers.

Following each interview, a traditional gift was presented to the participant. ISS was conducted according to each participant's schedule. Questions and guidelines were used to connect the dots in an open-ended manner so that the flow of the conversation was not interrupted. Participants were visited again if additional information was needed.

Photovoice

Photovoice has the potential to enable participants to depict people and places that are important to them within their land, home, education, and wider community (Adams et al., 2012; Darbyshire et al., 2005; Datta et al., 2015). Photography also offers a direct way of seeing the world and provides a valuable, visual component in a PAR methodology (Baker & Wang, 2006). Baker and Wang (2006) further state that photovoice creates different ideas for both adults and youth than those derived from verbal or written interviews. In this research, youth and coresearcher participants were requested to take pictures of their home, plants, animals, birds, land, the moon, rocks, and so on, and then shared the stories connected to their particular pictures. For this purpose, a digital camera was provided to participants. The printed pictures were given to participants for sharing their stories so that pictures could be used in the data analysis. Photovoice was also used in sharing circle and individual storytelling. The printed pictures were given to participants for sharing their stories followed by a consent form so that pictures could be used in this research. As part of the data-collection process, participants were invited to share photovoice entries via Facebook to be analyzed together with additional data.

Commonplace books

Commonplace books are helpful for collecting personal experiences, feelings, ongoing interaction among the researcher and participants, and any other information related to traditional culture (e.g., poems, photographs, drawings, etc.) (Sumara, 1996). I learned how to maintain a commonplace book during my coursework in EFDT 885: Investigations in Culture and Environment at the University of Saskatchewan. Unlike a journal, a commonplace book is meant to engage individuals in everyday activities in their place; these places can be cultivated land, forest, playgrounds, houses, waterfalls, local schools, and so on. A commonplace book represents a space where one can represent a variety of experiences in a variety of forms.

The use of commonplace books was an exciting and engaging method used in this research. It helped to build trusting relationships with the participants. Participants appreciated this process because they found it to be the first opportunity in their lives to write stories about themselves in their own words. Most Elders and Knowledge-holders wanted to have an opportunity to share their stories, but I had to limit participation in the use of commonplace books to participants who could both read and write. Due to a lack of Khyeng Indigenous script, we (the Elders, Knowledge-holders, coresearcher participants, and I) came to a decision that a commonplace book would be given to the four coresearcher participants because they were able to read and write in the Bangla language. Nevertheless, both Elders and Knowledge-holders agreed to share their knowledge with coresearcher participants for sharing in the coresearchers' commonplace books. Traditional gifts and honorarium followed each month for each coresearcher participant's commonplace book. The commonplace book was returned to the participants after data analysis.

Participant observation

Participant observation in this research was a significant challenge to Western ways of conducting participant observation. The participants were the researchers for conducting participant observation in this book research. Participant observation allows researchers to gather data on physical surroundings and human interactions and in engaging settings in their own land, relationships, and culture (Cohen et al., 2000; Patton, 1990, 2002). A major advantage of direct participant observation is that it provides in-depth, here-and-now experience to reveal implicit practices. According to Lincoln and Guba (1985), "observation . . . allows the inquirer to see the world as his subjects see it, to live in their time frames, to capture the phenomenon in and on its own terms, and to grasp the culture in its own natural, ongoing environment" (p. 273). Others have explained participant observation through participants as a tool that can be used to verify what has been shared through other tools such as traditional sharing circle, individual story sharing, commonplace book, and photovoice (Datta et al., 2015).

Coresearcher participants observed their friends, Elders, and other community villagers in Jhum and plain-land fields, homes, forest, local lakes, schools, as well as in various government and nongovernmental projects (e.g., tobacco plantations, lumber plantation, Brickfield, and tobacco burning place). Additionally, coresearcher participants and I observed conversations and TSC discussions to help understand and interpret the participants' expressions and responses. Although I was facilitating the discussions, I paid attention to what was being said and not said.

A participatory methodology of data analysis

An inductive coding process was applied in the analysis. An inductive approach was used "to discover the meaning that people award to their social worlds and to understand the meanings of their social behaviour" (Boeije, 2010, p. 12). In other words, rather than using a set of predetermined codes, the codes were inductively drawn from the data based on the content therein. Sharing research results and data analysis were significant parts of this research project. Field notes, commonplace books, documents, sharing circle data, and individual story sharing data were all transcribed through a collective process with the four Khyeng coresearcher participants. Transcribed data was also reviewed and shared with other participants through both individual and collective processes. Key terms and significant issues for data analysis were identified through a collective contribution process by the Elders, leaders, Knowledge-holders, and youth during a subsequent traditional sharing circle. Participants wanted to be sure their needs and dreams were included in the draft findings so that this research could have an impact on the policy level and speak on behalf of them.

The first stage of data analysis involved the non-Indigenous researcher and four Indigenous coresearcher participants reading through and viewing all of the data (transcribed story circles and individual stories, photos, and commonplace books). We divided our transcribed story circles and individual story data sets among the five of us for the coding process so that we all had an opportunity to examine each transcribed data set. We each noted keywords that represented the ideas in the data. Upon reaching more than 250 keywords collectively, we shared and compared our keywords and created a shared codebook that included a range of themes found in the data. We then revisited all of the data using these shared keywords to code themes according to the frequency of occurrence of keywords and "ordered [them] in subordinate and subordinate outline format to reflect on their possible groupings and relationships" (Saldana, 2010, p. 142). Photovoice keywords and themes were also identified through a similar sharing process. After identifying themes from story circles, individual stories, and photos, the coresearchers identified keywords and themes in the commonplace book data.

The next stage of data analysis involved sharing codes with the Elders and Knowledge-holders. The Elders and Knowledge-holders were asked to add and change any information that they thought was significant for this research. When new themes were suggested that were not represented in the original list of inductive codes, these were added to the codebook. After confirming themes with Elders and Knowledge-holders, we used a pattern-coding method to build keywords and themes into subpatterns and larger patterns. In pattern coding we reviewed our first cycle's themed codebook to assess themes' commonalities and determine subpatterns, which we then grouped into larger umbrella patterns. In identifying a pattern code we focused on understanding the whys, whats, and hows of how themes were interrelated and interdependent. We identified thirty-four subpatterns in eight larger patterns (see Table 3.1). In presenting the findings of the study, we used quotes from our conversations with Elders, Knowledge-holders, leaders, youth, and coresearcher participants. To maintain the authenticity and integrity of the data, we presented the quotes (English translation through coresearcher participants with participants' consent) verbatim as spoken by participants. Our commitment was to working relationally within the framework of the Indigenous community rather than the traditional research framework of the researcher taking away the material and identifying the codes. Through our relational PAR we learned that PAR researchers strive to break down the power hierarchy that is so prevalent in more traditional research (Adams et al., 2012; Chataway, 1997; Dei, 1999; Simpson, 2001). We wanted participants to view themselves as the experts and to recognize their power to create change.

We interpreted our relational PAR as collaborative ways of learning among Indigenous researchers, non-Indigenous researchers, community Elders, Knowledge-holders, and youth, such as: participatory ways of writing, analyzing, and disseminating research results. The core values, beliefs, and spiritual practices of the participant community were incorporated throughout the research process.

Table 3.1 Pattern and subpattern coding. Pattern coding undertaken through a participatory process (participants included the researcher, Khyeng Indigenous Elders, Knowledge-holders, and coresearcher participants) building on the first cycle of themed coding.

Pattern Coding	Subpattern
Khyeng Indigenous Meanings and Definitions	• Understanding of Land, Water, and Management • Land and Water Management
Traditional Land Practices	Modes of Land Distribution • Karbary, Headmen, Raja Modes of Food Distribution • Consumption and Market
Spirituality	• Land, Water, and Cultivation
Bangladesh Government's Land-Management Policies and Practices	Land Management Reserve Forest Policies • Profitable Plantations (Lumber) • Tobacco Plantations • Brickfield
Land Grabbing, Deforestation, and Poverty	Reasons • Bengali Settlement Policies (after 1972) • Brickfield • Profitable Plantation • Money Lending and Micro-Credit (Social Business) Exploitation
Hope to Protect Khyeng Cultivation Culture	Hopes for • Traditional Customary Land Rights and Practices • Khyeng Education (e.g., at least up to grade five)
Youth Sense of Activities to Protect Place (Land or Water)	Youth Activities • Learning Language and Cultivation Culture • Protecting Water, Animals, Plants, and Birds • Learning Land-Water Policies • Growing Food • Learning Stories and Spirituality from Elders
Dreams for Achieving Sustainability through Participatory and Collective Processes	Being Part of the Land-Water Management Policies and Decision-Making Processes in CHT • Forest Department, Reserve Forest Department, Indigenous Cultural Department, Land Reform Policy Department, and Education Institute • NGO Development, Research, and Policies

Community-based research ethics

This book's research followed both community and formal university research ethics. Formal ethical guidelines as set out by the Social Sciences and Humanities Research Council of Canada (2010) were strictly adhered to. I clearly explained and discussed the purpose of the research with the participants. I explained the expectations in terms of work and time commitments while letting the participants decide the appropriate times to meet.

Given the violent political situation in Bangladesh and the vulnerability of the Laitu Khyeng Indigenous community in the context of this social and political unrest, the anonymity as well as confidentiality of the research participants was of paramount importance. Therefore, every possible measure was taken to protect participants' identities. For example, participants' names were concealed with pseudonyms, and their geographic location used as a pseudonym if they so chose. Documented data such as interviews, transcripts, and field notes did not carry name identification. In the commonplace books, coresearcher participants' names were well documented according to their request. The interviews were audiotaped, transcribed, and translated, then safely locked away from the research sites, and one copy of the data set was given to the community's leader. There were not any foreseeable risks in terms of privacy and confidentiality because there was no public access to the raw data except by the Laitu Khyeng Indigenous participants. Individual participants were free in any situation and at any time to remove themselves from the research and/or remove their consent. Participants willingly participated and conducted the research. The consent process was a continuous process according to the participants' culture. Local participants individually and collectively discussed and were informed of any potential threat and dangers from the sharing of knowledge.

Direct quotations from the discussions and conversations were used in the research publications and presentations with participants' consent. To assure confidentiality of participants in the research, some names were replaced by pseudonyms. Participants were given the opportunity to choose their own pseudonym should they so wish. Original copies of all data will be kept for a minimum of five years and will then be destroyed.

This research recognized the value of Indigenous perspectives and their contribution to the research. The knowledge and experiences of Indigenous Elders and Knowledge-holders were treated with full respect. Participants discussed that this research would not direct benefits to the participants; however, participants would share ownership of the research results and publications. Coresearcher participants have been coauthors of post-research publications (Datta et al., 2015), and the community can access the research results, including prints, audio, video, and digital materials, at any time. All research reports and publications are available to the communities and individuals through their community leaders.

Safety was an important issue in conducting research with Bangladeshi CHT Indigenous communities due to the attitudes of Bangladeshi mainstream settlers and the Bangladeshi government's militarization (Human Right Report, 2013). However, building trustful relationships with Elders and Knowledge-holders created safe spaces for research in the Indigenous communities (Datta et al., 2015).

Responsibilities and benefits in PAR

A number of key responsibilities in participatory action research (PAR) play significant roles in both decolonizing our fixed ways of knowing and redistributing research power amongst Indigenous participants (Battiste, 2008; Wilson, 2008).

As noted earlier, key responsibilities include empowering participants, building trustful relationships, recognizing spiritual relationships, honoring relational and holistic knowledge, taking a political stand in support of the participants, and centering the Indigenous voice.

Empowering participants

In a relational PAR methodology, one of the main goals is to empower participants (Christopher et al., 2008). Empowerment is a process of building reciprocal relationships between researchers and participants (Meyer, 2001). Empowering participants emphasizes the researcher's responsibility toward participants rather than "being hierarchical, vertical, dominating, and exploitative" (Kesby, 2005, p. 2051). In this vein, Indigenous scholar Battiste (2008) suggests that the research should transfer power through the researcher's respect and accountability to the participants, particularly in Indigenous communities. Similarly, Tuck (2009) suggests research with Indigenous communities needs to be a process of reclaiming knowledge and redistributing power among participants. Using PAR with Indigenous communities may reduce inequality of power between participants and researchers. Thus, we suggest that PAR may be helpful in building a community's capacity in a way that values participant voices (Cahill, 2007).

To explore these foci, the Indigenous community Elders, leaders, Knowledge-holders, youth, and coresearcher participants developed methods and approaches to support their interests and participation. They shared their stories among their community members and interviewed individuals (sometimes their own relations) whom they identified as potential key actors (through their network). We realized that centering Indigenous voices through the relational PAR framework helped us to shift the power dynamic between the non-Indigenous researcher and the participants' community, particularly community Elders and Knowledge-holders who were involved in the study and interpreting findings. We found that such involvement was not only helpful in reducing power differences between the researchers and participants but that it also gave participants power to decide data quality.

Knowledge ownership

In this relational PAR study, knowledge ownership was seen as the most significant factor for building trustful relationships with the participants and the community. As participants in a collaborative research process (between a non-Indigenous researcher and Indigenous coresearcher participants), we learned that the researcher should play the role of interpreter and share research ownership with the community. For example, one of our participant Knowledge-holders explained how the existing (i.e., nonrelational) research became oppressive to them.

> There are a number of researchers who came to our community for research from various organizations (such as, the government, NGOs, research organizations, and universities) promising that they would bring many

positive changes for us, but once they [outside researchers] are done with their research, they never come back. In most cases, we did not even see our research results and/or research report. We do not know what information they have taken from us and for what. Both the nonrelational research and researchers are like *foreign birds* (those who come to our community only for their own interests) to us. They (both the nonrelational research and researchers) are nothing but oppression on our community. We are so upset with this kind of research on us. If it continues like this, we, as the Indigenous community, will never be able to get benefits from the research and researcher.

Despite these challenges, the Elder explained his expectations of the research and researcher. He said, "We need both research and non-Indigenous researchers in our Indigenous community, but they need to honor our knowledge and our spiritual practices. If their [outside researchers] research does not speak for our needs and create possibilities for us, why do we need research?" To address these concerns, we engaged in discussion with the community's Elder and leaders regarding ownership of knowledge (research) and the community's control over research data analysis. As a result of this transparency, the participants became friendlier, treated the (non-Indigenous) researcher as a community member, and helped to select community coresearcher participants for our research. Therefore, coownership of knowledge with the Indigenous community was an important issue with respect to building relationships with participants. Another Elder participant explained the benefits of this relational PAR by saying that "This PAR is different from other research because this PAR not only created a knowledge-sharing space for writing our own stories of oppression and suffering but also put our voice, our needs, and our abilities at its center."

Relationality

Relational accountabilities became a phenomenon for our PAR research. Relationships in PAR suggest a significant move from separate ways of being and doing (Baum et al., 2006; Datta et al., 2014; Dei, 2011; Torre & Ayala, 2009). Similarly, when PAR is interpreted through a relational ontology, everything is considered to have meaning, power, and agency (Hunington et al., 2006; Meyer, 2001; Tuck, 2009; Wilson, 2008). For example, in PAR, relationships are at the center of understanding the meanings of actors and actors' actions; all actions are a reflection of the previous actions of oneself and others (Latour, 1991). Thus PAR does not consider knowledge in Indigenous communities as a discrete entity; rather, knowledge is a relational and a holistic process (Johnson & Murton, 2007). For example, Glass and Kaufert (2006) suggest "certain stories may be of the community heritage. Or there may need to be recognition of an identified elder's ownership of some knowledge" (p. 34). Therefore, in recognizing participants' relationships, PAR plays a significant role in a relational ontology. We learned that the community's knowledge was intimately related to their ancestral relationships and their respect for this ancestry. Both the Elder and Knowledge-holder participants in our study described during our story sharing processes how the meanings of land and water interconnected. In addition, both were considered to be available for everyone. For example, the Elder Mong Shang Pure Khyeng explained in an individual sharing interview, "Everything in our community is relational such as: cultivated land, uncultivated land, food production, water, birds, animals, hills, sky, winds, insects, plants, trees, feelings, spirituality, sounds, father, mother, brother and sister, and others." Similarly, another Elder, Okko Khyeng, emphasized in a sharing circle, "All things are mutually interconnected and interdependent with other things."

Researchers' relational accountabilities toward Indigenous participants, according to Getty (2010), can enable Indigenous people to participate as researchers in partnership with academic research. For example, in our study Elder Kosomopure Khyeng argued that "we need non-Indigenous researchers for us. But I think they should be responsible to us while they are doing research with us, such as including our research needs, respecting our Elders and Knowledge-holders, and including us in the research process." Accordingly, the leaders see responsibilities as relational and respectful collaborations "among universities, government, non-Indigenous researchers, and Indigenous people." Similarly, we discovered that if a researcher could be respectful and supportive of relationships that had been established through the research process and personal relationships, a number of tensions between the researcher(s) and participants could be minimized.

Holism

Holism was another useful component of our relational PAR. Through holism we learned that a person was the sum (and more) of their many parts, including the spiritual, physical, cogitative, and emotional. We experienced holism as the four kinds of spirits, which could be transformed into protectors for the community's land, people, animals, and forest. Such spirits determine the community's everyday relational and spiritual practices in their forest and plain land. The meanings of management to the Indigenous community were considered to be everything. The Elder explained that the community's holism consisted of their "everyday relational practices." He explicitly described their holism as involving many relational and spiritual things' stories. These things' stories are "interconnected with their [the community members'] everyday practices; they include stories associated with forests, types of crops, the sun, the moon, sound, wind, relationships, spirituality, cultivation tools, and domestic animals," according to the Knowledge-holder. The traditional stories in their Indigenous community were interconnected with their everyday practices.

Centering Indigenous voices

Through conducting research in a participatory action research (PAR) framework and sharing the data-analysis process with coresearcher participants, Elders, and Knowledge-holders, it became evident that sharing data analysis was an active process for both the participants and the researcher because participants appeared to take ownership of their research findings. This PAR data-analysis process made a space for participants to dream and sustain hopes of saving their motherland and water. While participating in PAR, participants wanted to be sure their needs and dreams were included in the draft findings so that this research would have an impact at the policy level and speak on their behalf. Involving coresearchers, Elders, and Knowledge-holders in the data analysis also helped to ensure the trustworthiness of the themes by ensuring that the identified themes matched the understandings and interpretations of community members (Denzin & Lincoln, 2008). Thus, the conclusions resulting from our data analysis have been drawn based on this engagement process among us (non-Indigenous researcher and Indigenous coresearcher participants), Elders, and Knowledge-holders. The process was carried out in accordance with the community's needs, and aimed to address significant issues for their land-management practices and sustainability. The utmost effort was devoted to attempting to align with participants' expressed needs and hopes as determined in discussion between the participants and the researchers.

In our study, the participant community had full access to the collected data set. The interviews were audio-recorded and transcribed, then safely locked away within a secure location on the research sites. Two copies of data were kept. One digital copy was saved with a Khyeng Indigenous Elder with external hard drive, and a second copy was saved with the supervising researcher.

Through our PAR we learned that the Laitu Khyneg community peoples had been fighting to stop different agencies' unwanted development projects (e.g., lumber plantation, reserve forest, tobacco plantations, and Brickfield industrial companies) and protect their Mother Nature. We found that the relational PAR was helpful in exploring how the Laitu Khyneg Indigenous community had been dreaming, hoping, and working hard to rebuild their traditional forest-water management as part of their responsibilities for sustainability. Through our PAR, we also learned that this community not only had the ability to build a self-sufficient economy and protect its ecosystem but was also able to contribute to the Bangladeshi economy and create new forms of sustainability practices.

Our relational PAR and the participant guidelines helped us to minimize risks of harm. Three steps were taken to minimize risks of harm: sharing individual transcripts, editing ability, and data analyzing and sharing opportunities. We as researcher and coresearchers realized that the researcher's main responsibility was to minimize harm as far as possible.

Despite minimizing harm from our research, we were able to publish (through a research organization, Association for Land Reform and Development, Dhaka, Bangladesh, fund that works mostly for Indigenous communities) the coresearcher participants' commonplace books in book format, according to participants' wishes. This commonplace book was the first writing in the Khyeng community's own words, and the Khyeng coresearchers received a great amount of appreciation for their contribution. This book was distributed among the Bangladeshi government's Indigenous Ministry, Land Ministry, Forest Ministry, UNDP, ILO, numerous research organizations, and universities abroad (Datta et al., 2015).

We also learned through our PAR that this community not only had the ability to build a self-sufficient economy and protect its ecosystem but that it was also able to contribute to the Bangladeshi economy and create new forms of sustainability practices. We saw firsthand that the Laitu Khyneg Indigenous community had been working hard to rebuild their traditional sustainability.

In summary, through our relational PAR we found that the researcher's responsibilities to the participants' community opened many possibilities. The researcher's responsibilities were to actively engage with participants' empowerment, needs, relationality, spirituality, and holism. Thus, like Ferreira and Gendron (2011), we would like to argue that when conducting research with Indigenous communities, the researcher needs to consider each participant's knowledge as significant and worthy of respect; in fact, researchers using PAR may want to consider each participant as a "coresearcher and co-learner" (p. 157). Indeed, our experiences showed that using PAR in our study was not only helpful for us in exploring the richness of the Laitu Khyeng Indigenous cultures (for sharing, teaching, analyzing, uncovering, and reclaiming knowledge) but also inspired us (both participants and researchers) to dream and hope.

Conclusion

Throughout this relational PAR research we learned that study was both a ceremony and a learning process (Wilson, 2008). The most important lesson learned from our experience of using a relational PAR research framework in academia was how the *rules* of academia and of research need not always allow a Western research framework to flourish. The application of a relational PAR research framework in academia is an important theoretical contribution and provides a different way of knowing, one that endeavors to decolonize both the research and researcher.

We hope that this research contributes to the growing scholarly work on bridging non-Indigenous researcher and Indigenous ways of knowing, in this case using a relational PAR approach. It is our hope that future non-Indigenous researchers will use methods that not only respect and honor Indigenous ways of knowing but are also based on collaboration, Indigenous needs, hopes, and knowledge.

Outline of remainder of this chapter

This chapter has described the research approaches that I used to explore how land, management, and sustainability were taken up in the forms of knowledge and practice embedded in the local culture of Laitu Khyeng Indigenous community. A participatory action research methodology was employed in the study. Coresearcher participants were a vital part of this research. Elders, Knowledge-holders, leaders, and youth were the research participants. Data were collected through the traditional sharing circle, individual story sharing, photovoice, commonplace books, and observations. Following an inductive data analysis, four themes were identified which I present in the next four chapters.

Notes

1 Some parts of this chapter were previously published in the *International Journal of Social Research Methodology* (Datta,R., Khyang, N., Khyang, K. H., Kheyang, P. Khyang, C. M., & Chapola, J., 2015). Reprint permission received.
2 The term *we* refers collectively to the research team and the collective ways of conducting research as part of participatory action research (PAR). Although this book's author is single author, this book's research is contacted through a collective process with Indigenous participants: Elders, Knowledge-holders, leaders, youths, and four coresearcher participants. *We*, as a collective research team, were continuously engaged and participated all through the field-research and data-analysis processes, such as: identifying research questions; facilitating traditional sharing circles; conducting participant observation and photovoice; recording traditional sharing circles and individual storytelling discussions; maintaining a commonplace book, which was used to record personal observations, art, poems, experiences, stories about the environment, field notes; and helping with coding and analyzing research data, etc. (Datta et al., 2015). The term *we* in this chapter refers as respect, honor, and reciprocal relationships with participant's community.
3 The university academic, non-Indigenous researcher and the Indigenous community's coresearcher participants.
4 This relational PAR research was a participatory research journey. We (university academic, non-Indigenous researcher, Indigenous participant community coresearchers, Elders, leaders, and Knowledge-holders) collectively identified research themes, collected research data, analyzed research results, and owned research results.
5 I use the term *minority* here to indicate non-Islamic communities such as Hindu, Buddhist, Christian, and various Indigenous communities (Human Right Congress for Bangladesh Minorities report, 2013). Minorities face many difficulties in equal land rights, policy-making, and education in Bangladesh (Human-Right Watch Report, 2011). Minorities are often displaced from their original land, oppressed in their everyday practices, and excluded from any kind of major decision-making process in relation to their land (Internal Displacement Monitoring Centre Report, 2016; Iva, 2010).

4 Traditional meanings of land-water

This chapter discusses theme one: traditional land-water customs and practices. Two emergent Indigenous environmental issues are discussed in this chapter through ethnographic participatory action research (PAR): (1) the community's perceptions of land-water meanings, and (2) the community's understanding of traditional environmental management (through the agriculture domain,[1] traditional modes of administrative structure,[2] spirituality, and the traditional economy). In data collected across the various research methods employed in the study – sharing circles, individual story sharing, coresearcher commonplace books, and participant observation – participants suggested that land, water, and traditional management are integrated and interconnected within everyday practices. The research findings corresponding to each subtheme emerging in theme one are discussed in the following sections.

The community's perceptions of land-water meanings

One of the central themes evident in the data relating to current and past traditional land and water practices is that of meanings associated with land and water. In explaining the community's orientations to land and water, the research participants, particularly Elders and Knowledge-holders, highlighted interconnectedness, spirituality, belongingness, identity, respect, honor, sacredness, and ritual. These issues are discussed next.

A significant issue that arose in participants' discussions about land and water was the **interconnectedness** of the two. During our first sharing circle and individual story-sharing process, both Elders and Knowledge-holders suggested that the meanings of land and water are linked. For example, Elder Kosomo Pure Khyeng explained

> Land and water are everything for us, such as: our cultivated land, uncultivated land, food production, water, birds, animals, hills, sky, wind, insects, plants, trees, feelings, spirituality, sounds, father, mother, brother and sister, and others. Land and water are for us both visible and invisible things. Visible things are human, animals, birds, crops, lands, insects, mountains, rocks, the moon, sun, water, and so on. Invisible things are our feelings, wind, smells, sounds, and spirituality.

Participants, particularly Elders and Knowledge-holders, emphasized respect and honor, spiritual practices, and responsibilities as facets of this interconnectedness. Elders and Knowledge-holders explained that they enjoy interconnected collective practices with land and water as they (community) engage physically, emotionally, economically, socially, culturally, and spiritually. Another important issue discussed by Elders and Knowledge-holders was that land and water knowledge are not static but change over time as the community's cultivation culture changes.

A related focus in the data was on the significance of **spirituality**. In Khyeng, spirits are considered as different forms of practices that offer protection through the community's everyday relationships. Knowledge-holder Kasamong Prue Khyeng[3] explained that protection was viewed as being offered through four spirits (see Figure 4.1): the sun spirit, the land and water spirit, the nature spirit, and the exchange spirit. The sun spirit represents a number of gods: the water god, the wind god, the hill god, the sky god, and the moon god. Similarly, the nature spirit is a combination of the cultivation god, the animal god, the cultivation tools god, the crop god, and the bird god. The land and water spirit corresponds with the plant god, the animal god, the water god, the land god, and the insect god. Finally, the exchange spirit links with the crisis relief god, the equal distributions god, the sharing god, the food god, and the market god. Elder Basa Khyang provided further detailed articulation about the relationship between meanings of land-water and spirituality, emphasizing his perception of land and water as "everyday spiritual practices" and that "The meanings of land and water are our things' spiritual prayers: they are our protectors." A significant point we learned from our sharing circles and individual interview processes was that each spirit was considered a vital actor toward illuminating the community's cultivation culture and customs; all of these spirits were divinely interconnected and they determined the community's everyday relational and spiritual practices in their forested and deforested[4] lands.

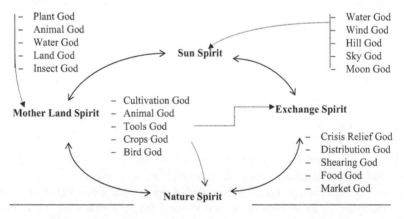

Figure 4.1 Land, water, and spirituality spirits. This figure developed based on participants' relational and spiritual stories.

According to participants, land and water are also understood in terms of **belongingness** in Khyneg culture. For instance, Elder Okko Khyeng explicitly stated in the first sharing circle: "Land and water do not belong to us; we belong to them. However, we can share our land and water collectively. For us, both of them are our parents" (Figure 4.2). He further stressed the collective sharing process as follows: "Our beautiful land and water are our parents and our heart. We believe our land and water have created us. We cannot survive without each other." According to this understanding, land and water are a part of the collective rights, based on a relationship with nature. Therefore, land and water are credited with establishing belonging relationships among Khyeng members, animals, plants, and fish.

Many of the sharing circle participants spoke about their ties with local land and water and explained how their ties represent their Indigenous **identity**. Participants discussed that land and water were central to the community's beliefs, identity, and cultural values. For example, Elder Okko Khyeng expressed the following: "Our land and water talk for us. Our land, water, forest, animals are all about who we are."

The community's everyday land and water practices were also articulated in relation to **respect** (i.e., recognizing every animal and plant species has a significant purpose in the environment). For example, Elders and Knowledge-holders

Figure 4.2 Water spirituality: *Water does not belong to us; we belong to the water.* Elder Okko Khyeng. "Our water talks for us. Our water is all about who we are." Coresearcher Nyojy U Khyang. This PhD research photo represents water as indigenous identity. The community sees water as central to its beliefs, identity, and cultural values.

suggested that respect was an important point for explaining their land and water to the community. Elders and Knowledge-holders explained that crop production and animal husbandry were interdependent in the mixed farming systems of the community. Animals are hugely important to the economy considering their roles in transportation, land cultivation, and providing manure for fuel and fertilizer. As a symbol of respect, most families raise cattle as an essential component of their management system. Since dairy cows are directly linked to family income, nutrition, and welfare, the community views cows as intimately connected with the cultivation god(s). Although animals are a part of the mixed farming system, the goal of their integration is not the maximization of material gains. Rather, participants expressed that the goal is to practice respect for the value of all living and nonliving components of the environment.

To explain the meanings of land and water, both Elders and youth drew on descriptions of **honor practices**. Coresearcher Nyojy U Khyang provided an example in his commonplace book: "When we climb up a big tree for food, we pray and ask permission from the plant by saying, 'Do you allow me to take your creation [fruits] for us?'" He proceeded to explain that "The community believes if they ask permission from the trees, they are indicating that the community will not overuse their resources, and then the trees will continue blessing the community." Nyojy U Kjuang shared this sentiment in the prayer, "We will not hurt you and will not take more than we need." Similarly, Elder Okko Khyeng stated during sharing circle that

> The land and water are our teachers who teach us how to honor our land and water gods. We have many lands and water gods, such as: *Lokhei, Bogle, Siksi, Khamotto, Shoila Siksi*, and *Mina* [names of land and water gods], whom we pray to and respect every day. In our gods'[5] names we sacrifice our domestic animals. We believe our relational land and water gods will protect us from various crises and provide us with food.

Land and water were also indicated as significant sources of **ritual**. Ritual was discussed in relation to seeing the land and water as alive and as associated with honoring ancestors. For example, we learned that many people in the community started their day by praying to the forest, land, and water gods and Elders. They believed that if they did not respect and honor the land and water, the ancestors would not protect them during food crises and sickness.

Traditional land-water knowledge is not merely practices to the Indigenous community – they think their knowledges have the scientific basis for their community's environmental sustainability because they have been living in their land-water for thousands of years. Therefore, they believe that their traditional scientific knowledge is significant for the whole ecosystem and can contribute to future meanings of sustainability for the state and beyond.

The community explained land and water were **sacred places** for the community. The community saw them as part of creation. Participants suggested they think they were created by land and water. The community used the word **sacred** as a sign of care. In other words, sacred was a word used to convey the special care taken with the land and water. Sacred was also discussed as a connector between spirituality and practice. For example, Elder Kosomo Prue Khyeng said that "Since our land [father] and water [mother] are as our parents, we have sacred responsibilities to care [for] our parents [land and water]." He also believed that "What we do to the land and water today impacts on what happens to the environment in the future." Thus, the term sacred has significant meaning in the community's everyday management practice.

The Laitu Khyeng Indigenous Elder showed land and water as sacred places and his perception with a poem (translated by coresearcher participant Mathui Ching Khyang).

> O our beautiful Mother forest, land, and water,
> You are the great divine power.
> We are devoted to you
> You are in our heart; please do not leave us.
> Protect us and keep us in your blessings.
> Give us strength so that we can protect ourselves.

To understand traditional meanings of land and water, it is evident that Elders and Knowledge-holders positioned their understanding in relation to everyday knowledge and practices. The data suggest that the community's attitude towards land and water consists of an obligation to care, honor, and learn about land and water and a sense that they are connected spiritually to land and water in their everyday practices. In other words, understandings of land and water are interconnected with everyday life (further elaborated under subtheme two).

This study acknowledges the importance of the community's traditional understandings and practices of land-water practices (Battiste, 2000; Deyhle, 2009; Tuck & McKenzie, 2015). The study's findings reveal that the participants valued knowledge of Indigenous everyday practices when it came to explanations of the community's perceptions of land-water.

Hybrid practices

The concept of hybridity has been one of the most powerful means of reexamining and reconfiguring everyday practices in a way that values diversity and honors interconnectedness among multiple actors (Ashcroft et al., 1998; Whatmore, 2002, 2006). In postcolonial literature, hybridity has been given varied meanings and has been applied in a variety of ways (Forsyth, 1996). To explore everyday practices, Kraidy (2002) emphasized the concept of hybridization. Kraidy (2002) outlined that at the level of the everyday, we are confronted with a network of complex relationships, dynamic and process-based practices that constitute hybrid realities. Thus, meanings and practices of land and water as hybrid realities emphasize a plurality that recognizes diversity, interconnectivity, identity, and strengths (Dove, 2006; Amoamo & Thompson, 2010).

60 Traditional meanings of land-water

From a foundation of hybridity, we cannot create a separation between human and nonhuman actors (Latour, 2004). Bhabha's (2004) writings on hybridity have been important in articulating Laitu Khyeng land and water understandings and practices because his conceptualization makes it clear that the community's land and water must be understood as complex integrations of multiple meanings, historical temporalities, and positions. Other writers are equally insistent on this; for example, Pieterse (2004, p. 82) wrote that "hybridity is as fluid, the mixing of culture, rather than their separateness is emphasized." In our research findings, the community's perspectives on hybridity also offer empowerment through acknowledging the correlation between traditional knowledge and everyday practices as an integral part of their Indigenous identity. For example, Elder Kosomo Prue Khyeng identified that land and water have multiple interconnected meanings to the community, such as parents, friends, and god(s). Likewise, Knowledge-holder Kasamong Prue Khyeng discussed the multiple meanings of land and water through describing four kinds of spirits, all having different but interrelated purposes (see Figure 4.1). Therefore, in hybridity, community's traditional land-water knowledge is considered as scientific knowledge (see Figure 4.3).

In the Laitu Khyeng context, hybrid understandings of land and water are significant for the community's land rights and identity. Such a correlation seeks to advance the discussion of Bhabha's concept of hybridity as a means of understanding the transformative and dynamic interplay of cultural land practice. For example, as Elder Kosomo Prue Khyeng explained, "For us, both land and water are our parents, culture, and our identity."

Figure 4.3 Water knowledge. "Our land-water knowledge is scientific knowledge for our community," said Elder Kosomo Pure Khyeng from the Laitu Khyeng Indigenous community in Chittagong Hill Tracts (CHT), Bangladesh.

To the Laitu Khyeng Indigenous community, hybrid meanings of land and water are connected to their strength (Bhabha, 2004, 1996). Consequently, notions of hybridity are conveyed discursively through community operations to establish this strength. For example, Knowledge-holder Ching Cho Khyeng characterized traditional land and water practices as sustainable management practice. The Knowledge-holder further stated, "Our natural crisis [which is not imposed] is also our strength as our crisis also teaches us how to face challenging situations."

Thus, we can see that to the Laitu Khyeng community, hybrid notions of land and water are complex and diverse. Ideas of hybridity presented by Bhabha (1994), Latour (2004), and Whatmore (2006) illuminate the multiple complexities involved in community land and water practices, decentering colonial orientations that privilege fixity and rigidity. Laitu Khyeng notions of land and water hybridity offer the opportunity to rethink how to move beyond fixed, dominant perspectives that are entrenched in a colonial Eurocentric framework. Thus, hybrid meanings illuminate Laitu Khyeng land and water understandings and practices within the possibilities of diversity, interconnectivity, identity, and strength.

Spiritual and relational

In addition to hybrid meanings of land and water, study participants also wanted to highlight the theme of **relationality**. Relationality is significant for the community's identity and other rights. The role of relationality in understanding the meanings of land and water can be explained symbolically in that it centers around Indigenous rights and their lives (Escobar, 2008; Wilson, 2008). In this study, participants' relational understandings and practices of land and water use have strong theoretical implications: namely, relationships with the community are alive and have agency, and relationality centers on Indigenous voices and needs.

The Laitu Khyeng Indigenous communities view their spiritual and relational management practices with the environment as having scientific and ecological significance. The researchers identified examples from the participant discussions, photovoice, and commonplace books in which Laitu Khyeng Indigenous management practices offered solutions to multiple ecological and sociological issues. We discovered that traditional spiritual and relational management can reduce species extraction, water crises, logging, weeds, and food crises and that traditional management knowledge increases diversity in plant and animal species, decision-making power among woman, youth empowerment, production of organic fertilizers, crop selection, and surplus distribution. Participants also expressed that common and scientific meanings of management practices are essential for reconstructing the Laitu Khyeng Indigenous identity, culture, and sustainable livelihood. Such a narrative can offer the opportunity to reconstruct, communicate, and reclaim Laitu Khyeng Indigenous traditional practices of natural resource management. On a similar note, Berkes (2003) discussed Indigenous traditional management practices as scientific knowledge. The author explained that Indigenous traditional knowledge promotes the protection of remaining components of biodiversity and the unique values of local cultures; in addition, it can enhance the ability of local communities to establish a livelihood.

Indigenous scholar Simpson (2001) suggested that, in the Indigenous worldview, everything is alive, sacred, and relational. He theorized that human, nonhuman, and spiritual relationships were indispensable to Indigenous worldviews. Similarly, analysis of the data showed that to the study participants all human and nonhuman relationships are alive and have agency. For instance, participants discussed that relationships represent the foundation of help, support, and respect for spirituality, environment, natural law, and traditional cultivation culture. With such a connection, Koukkanen (2000) emphasized the relational agency of respect and honor within Indigenous worldviews. He explained that Indigenous respect for land and water is grounded in understanding and honoring relationships, which empowers a consideration that everything is equal, albeit different, and interdependent. In a similar manner, Greenwood (2009) suggested that relationships are powerful, significant, and complex: relationships are all about "deconstructing and reconstructing identities" (p. 277). In the data, participants explained that land and water constitute a relational space for the community. For example, coresearcher participant Mathui Ching Khyeng wrote the following in her commonplace book: "Our relationships with our land and water are like our parents who can take care of our everyday needs, teach us, protect us, and guide us."

Indigenous people position relational practices of land and water as central to communicate their culture, spirituality, production, consumption, and economy (Escobar, 2008 Meyer, 2001). Other Indigenous scholars – Kovach (2005, 2009) and Wilson (2008) – similarly position relationality as central to explaining Indigenous worldviews. According to Kovach, Indigenous ways of knowing and acting are dependent on relationality. Laitu Khyeng Elder Okko Khyeng expressed that relationality helps the community to be responsible not only for their lives but also for everything in their environment. Reinforcing the point, Knowledgeholder Ching Cho Khyeng stated, "Our relationality helps us to respect and honor our land and water gods. We believe our relationality guides us and inspires us to speak up for our land and water rights." He further explained, "Our relationships with our land and water not only speak for ourselves but also for our animals, species, plants, and so on. Thus, our relationships with our land and water can be seen as our needs. Indeed, we are here for our relationships."

In other words, traditional Indigenous land-water management practices and understandings are considered successful for natural resource management with respect to social, political, economic, and ecological domains. Bohensky and Maru (2011) also suggest that in seeking practical solutions to environmental and socio-economic impacts, local Indigenous management knowledge is a vital resource. Visions of community management can be seen as relational and scientific practices in opposition to the West. In addition, Indigenous and non-Indigenous scholars (Lertzman, 2010; Nadasdy, 1999; Escobar, 2010) explain that Indigenous people now engage with many decentralized approaches to environmental management, approaches that offer opportunities for integration of

Indigenous environmental management and Western science to promote cultural diversity within the management of social-ecological system sustainability.

In summation, Indigenous hybrid and relational understandings of land and water are vital to building trajectories of Indigenous resistance (Altman, 2009; Amoamo & Thompson, 2010; Tuck & McKenzie, 2015). Like Escobar (2008), we as researchers identified three reasons why hybrid and relational practices of land and water are needed for Indigenous identity, culture, justice, and sustainable living: first, traditional land and water knowledge generally connects with body, environment, culture, and economy in all of their diversity; second, land and water practices are continuous sources of culture and identity, which decolonize social life; and third, Indigenous land and water understandings and practices can restore traditional practice, and reconstitute today's cultural, economic, and ecological policies. Thus, like Smith (1999) in New Zealand, Wilson (2008) in Australia, Meyer (2008) in Hawaii USA, and Kovach (2009) in Canada, participants emphasized hybridity and relational understandings and practices of land and water in order to communicate and empower their traditional land and water practices. Aligned with trajectories of land-rights movements, this study prioritizes Laitu Khyeng Indigenous community's understanding and practices of land and water, their land and water rights movements, and their Indigenous identity.

In this chapter we can see the application of traditional Indigenous, practice-based meanings of land-water. We look forward to future evaluations of its general effectiveness in guiding practitioners and researchers of scientific and Indigenous knowledge integration in environmental management. We would like to see traditional cultivation culture and practices recognized as equivalent to the state management system. We have suggested that traditional meanings of land-water management rely on a community's traditional knowledge through their histories, contexts, values, culture, and worldviews, namely, of what Said calls the "imperialist dynamic" – the constant impulse to objectify, simply, and decontextualize people in the service of political and economic power (Said, 1993). A corollary to this is that Western environment management policies can benefit significantly from traditional meanings of land-water and environmental resource management.

Notes

1 According to the community's Elders and Knowledge-holders, the agriculture domain entails the community's food production and consumption, such as crops, cultivation tools, and natural resources.
2 Traditional administrative structure was explained by Elders, Knowledge-holders, and leaders as Indigenous (local) authority over Indigenous natural resource management, consumption, and life in CHT.
3 In some parts of this chapter we have enclosed participants' information and in some parts we have not disclosed participants' information in accordance with their requests.
4 Deforested land is known as plain land in the community (Adnan, 2004).
5 The term *god* is used to explain the community's spiritual belief in nature gods (e.g., the land gods, hill gods, water gods, stone gods, sun gods, animal gods).

5 The community's perceptions of meanings of management

This chapter answers some key challenges we face today: What can Western science learn from traditional land-water management? How can we bridge between Western and Indigenous land-water management? Do we have within us the necessary wisdom and knowledge to make this happen? To answer these questions, this chapter will focus on exploring the meanings of land-water and management from Indigenous people's everyday lives and their natural resource embodiment. For this, we begin by critically discussing the difference between the concepts of Western and Indigenous environmental management. In addition, we discuss how we as researchers have understood and used the Western concept of management in our paper. Furthermore, we discuss different agencies' management practices and challenges in the community that are relevant to this study. Moreover, we share participants' traditional meanings of management from their everyday practices. In our discussion section, we address why we, both as researchers and educators, need to redefine the meanings of management from the community's perspective and practices. Ultimately, Elders, Knowledge-holders, and youth participants guided us with techniques to establish traditional knowledge-oriented management. This type of management can benefit both state and local communities in long-term sustainability.

Laitu Khyeng Indigenous community's meanings of management

This chapter's theme, management, arose from the data analysis and addresses issues of traditional meanings of management in relation to local knowledge and practice. This section critically examines the difference between Western and Indigenous meanings of management and takes a stand for participants' perspectives on Indigenous meanings of management. To do this, we critically examine the difference between Western and Indigenous meanings of management and the community's perceptions on the meanings of management.

As previously discussed (see chapter 2), Western and Indigenous meanings of management carry fundamentally different meanings in terms of different worldviews with their own philosophy, practices, and methods (Lertzman, 2010; Lertzman & Vredenburg 2005). Studies (Clarkson et al., 1992) have identified certain of the Indigenous ways and means of reconnecting with ancestors and Indigenous understanding of their relationship to the Mother Earth. Traditional Indigenous meanings have alternative ways of protecting the Indigenous environment that are not only ways of reconnecting but are also healing ways for their animals, people, forest, and so on.

Indigenous meanings of practice (*management*) have diverse implications for the local people. The differences between Western and Indigenous knowledge practices were discussed with Elders, Knowledge-holders, leaders, and coresearcher participants, and we agreed to use the term *management* to describe the community's ways of understanding, practicing, and respecting their land, water, and environment. Participants wanted to use the Western term, management, as it is widely used in Bangladeshi state land and forest policies nationally and internationally. For example, Elder Basa Khyeng expressed in a telephone conversation, "We need to talk and use words the Bangladeshi government uses so that our government and international agencies will be able to understand the importance of our traditional cultivation practices." Thus, the research collective used the Western word, management, according to Elders', Knowledge-holders', and leaders' perceptions. Participants suggested that the community's understanding of land, water, and forest management are interconnected with a number of issues, such as the agriculture domain, traditional administration, spirituality, and traditional economy. This section examines the extent to which law (in particular, customary laws),[1] traditional institutions, and the rights of participation by Indigenous people are taken into account in natural resource management in the region. Our focus was not on understanding the Bangladesh government's meanings of management; rather, it was on understanding Indigenous meanings of management as embodied in Indigenous people's everyday lives. To explain the community's views on the theme of environmental management, each of the issues are elaborated below.

The agriculture domain

The agriculture domain was explained as a vital part of the community's environmental management practices. The community's traditional agricultural domain was conceptualized by participants as a web of inter-related and multidirectional relationships (see Figure 5.1) as specified during the first and second sharing circle

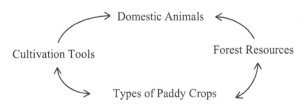

Figure 5.1 The agriculture domain. This figure was developed based on conversations with Elders and Knowledge-holders

discussions. Several significant interconnected aspects of the agriculture domain were discussed by study participants, including types of crops, forest resources, cultivation tools, and domestic animals.

Types of Paddy

Particular crops were discussed to have a major role in land and water management practices in the community. Elders and Knowledge-holders explained that a particular crop could be understood as a family member and could have an impact on other family members' actions (such as decision-making processes, cultivation, savings, and spiritual celebrations). The Elders explained that there are three kinds of paddy crops produced in the Khyeng community: *Binni* crop (mostly used in spiritual practices and on special occasions), Jhum crop[2] (for everyday use), and *plain-land*[3] crop (common paddy crop, which is similar to Jhum crop). To explain land, water, and forest management, participants discussed the meanings to the community of these three different types of paddy crops and how the different crops influenced everyday management practices.

The *Binni* paddy crop plays a crucial role in the community's harvest management. The Binni paddy crop was described by participants as a symbol of land fertility and of respect. First, participants suggested that the community believes that this symbol of land fertility increases land fertility generally across all forms of crop production. For example, the Khyeng community does not cultivate Jhum or plain-land crops without cultivating a Binni paddy crop. Knowledge-holder Ching Sho Khyeng indicated that Binni crop cultivation is seen as a way to maintain the health of different crops simultaneously. Second, growing a Binnip crop as a symbol of respect was explained in terms of the community's moral values.[4] Elder Kosomo Pure Khyeng discussed how the cultivation of a Binni crop contributes to the protection of land, water, and animals.

Similar to the Binni paddy crop, the Jhum crop also helps illuminate the community's land, water, and forest management practices. In his commonplace book, Hla Aung Prue Kyeng summarized Elders' and Knowledge-holders' description of Jhum functions. First, Jhum is central to a multiple-crop cultivation system, including different kinds of paddy crops, various types of vegetables, and many types of fruit and cash crops. The potential of the Jhum land to sustain multicrop food production ensures staple food and nutrients for the community. Second, the Jhum cultivation practices can help create new forests of traditional plants for other forest actors, such as mammals, birds, and insects. Third, the Jhum land crops act to protect large plants, particularly large trees growing on hilly slopes. Fourth, the Khyeng have certain rituals to control fire within Jhum land; such Jhum cultivation rituals not only control forest fires and protect forest animals but also provide ashes and fertilizer for future forest cultivation. Fifth, the Jhum crops are knowledge keepers; during Jhum cultivation, the Khyeng practice their traditional dancing, singing, storytelling, and poem reciting. The Jhum crops are considered a place of knowledge keeping[5] for the community. Finally, the Jhum crops help to encourage the practice of customary laws; the community practice Jhum cultivation according to the Khyeng's customary laws, such as traditional cultural practices, values, and cultivation.

Plain-land crops[6] are mainly grown in the plain land. According to Knowledge-holder Kosomo Prue Khyeng, almost 30% of the community's food comes from plain-land crops. Most of these are linked with local lake water, domestic animals, and fish. Elders explained in the second sharing circle that plain-land crops were not only considered a source of food production for Khyeng but also as sharing places for nonhuman beings, such as domestic animals (e.g., cattle, pigs, sheep), birds, and fish. In addition, plain-land crops were discussed as providing financial solvency[7] for the community.

In summary, participants emphasized that the various kinds of crops inform and require different forms of management, including being a source of the Khyeng community's inspiration for cultivation, a symbol of forest diversity and protection, and a symbol of cultural and financial security.

Forest resources

Forest resources are an important component of the community's land, water, and environment management systems. Elders and Knowledge-holders consider forest resources to include forested land and hilly land. To them, these forest resources provide many **gifts** (Elders explained these as opportunities) for the community's everyday management practices. These gifts include the space to grow edible vegetables and paddy crops, animals for hunting, bamboo for housing, and plants for medicine and spirituality. Traditional forms of management practices create equal accessibility for community members. For instance, community members have equal rights to the hilly land, Jhum, and water sources. This access helps the community to practice their ancestors' spirituality. Elders explained that these forms of access were helpful in creating two types of service in the community: exchange labor and appreciated labor. The exchange labor is characterized as a service. The term service was used by participants to explain different forms of labor, such as plain-land labor, Jhum-land labor, and house labor. This service is used to produce subsistence crops (e.g., ginger, vegetables, fruits, cotton, and animal foods) and paddy crops. The labor service is exchangeable for various other labor and/or cash arrangements. The second form of service, appreciated labor, is a form of gift. Various forms of labor are practiced, gifted, and consumed as a form of appreciation. Appreciation can be both respect and partial payment through non-monetary products such as rice or beer. This rice or beer offering can create long-term relationships among villagers in the form of entertainment or through expressions of respect.

In summary, participants indicated that forest resources were a major source of the community's food supply, agricultural cultivation, and economic well-being. As a result, forest cultivation plays a significant role in maintaining management practices in the community.

Cultivation tools

The land, water, and forest management practices are largely dependent on the community's traditional cultivation tools: the sword, the spear, and the knife. These three kinds of cultivation tools have different functions in the community's management practices.

The sword has two purposes in the community's environmental management, including ritual and inspiration. The ritual function, explained as gifts (i.e., forms of honor), are practiced during spiritual ceremonies such as those corresponding to marriage and harvest. For example, during marriage ceremonies the sword is used as a symbol of honor toward both the land and the new couple, and during harvest ceremonies, the sword is used as a form of inspiration. The inspiration is associated with the potential protection of family, forest, plants, land, water, and animals. However, in both cases, Khyeng community members do not sell their sword for monetary gain. The sale of a sword is described as dishonoring the family and the community's traditional values.

The spear is also used for various ceremonial purposes, such as rituals of honor, prestige, and respect. The social value of the spear to the community is greater than its cash value. The community considers the spear their protector. For example, one of the Elders stated, "We use our spear in our food cultivation and housework. We cannot go through a day without a spear." Like the sword, the Khyeng do not sell their spears. The rationale for not selling the spear is based on the inevitable loss of food production. However, the Khyeng community exchanges spears with other Indigenous communities as a nonmonetary form of trade. It is a symbol of honor and respect to their ancestors, land, and community.

Together with the sword and spear, the knife is considered a vital tool for environmental management. The knife is used as a gift in marriage ceremonies, as a symbol of hard work in Jhum land, and as a symbol of fertility for new families. According to custom, knives have to be kept in a high place as a symbol of power to protect the harvest and family from future crises. Although displayed as a prominent symbol, the knife is commonly used and not considered a commodity of monetary value to the community.

In summation, the data shows that the three cultivation tools have different kinds of influence on the community's management practices. First, the Elders and Knowledge-holders discussed that the sword and the spear symbolize the power of judgment for land distribution within the community. For example, sword and spear holders are considered respected and knowledgeable individuals. Second, the number of swords and spears are symbolic of the economic strength of the community. An abundance of sword and spear holders is related to a food surplus and therefore protection power. Third, the knives are a symbol of fertility and hard work.

All three cultivation tools (the sword, the spear, and the knife) are explained as symbols of empowerment for all genders, and all Khyeng have equal access during their everyday cultivation and ceremonial practices. The Khyeng men/women/others all have equal access to these tools, and all gender identities are welcome to participate in cultivation. For example, one of our coresearcher participants showed in their commonplace book that the Khyeng women produce food with their cultivation tools (i.e., sword, spear, and knife) and sell/exchange their produce in the village market. The Khyeng women can hold these tools and have major decision-making roles in family and community. Other non-Indigenous Bangladeshi people have different kinds of practice (Adnan, 2004).

Domestic animals

Domestic animals represent a significant component of the community's land, water, and forest management. The correlation between domestic animals and traditional management practices is described in the data as bestowing different degrees of social and economic prestige within the community. Having more domestic animals means more economic security, a more highly esteemed reputation, and more prestige for the entire family. However, because domestic animals are considered protector god(s) for the Khyeng, the conversion of domestic animals into monetary currency does not have equal meaning in terms of prestige and social reputation. During the research-gathering process, Elders clarified that different domestic animals have varied influence on the community's sense of management practices. Although the Khyeng did not traditionally sell their domestic animals for monetary gain often, their tradition has changed recently. At present, cattle, chicken, and goats have cash value in the local market and can be transformed into economic capital to obtain an education, daily goods, and labor for cultivation practices and other resource management. Elders pointed out that although the Khyeng practices concerning domestic animals have changed recently, the community is still spiritually connected with their domestic animals, including cattle, chickens, goats, and pigs, in their everyday life.

Cattle have multiple benefits within the community's everyday management practices and are able to protect them during times of crisis. For instance, cattle have many uses in the community's land and water practices, such as digging and plowing plain land for cultivation, producing dung for fertilizer and fuel, providing milk for food items, and being used in spiritual ceremonies.

The pig is another common domestic animal in the community. Domesticated pigs were described in the data as a gift that is exchangeable among the Khyeng or other Indigenous communities; however, the pig market is restricted within the intercommunity market due to the pork restriction observed by the Bangladeshi Muslim community. The pig is used in various cultivation ceremonies, such as Jhum celebrations, spiritual celebrations, and ceremonies around crop production. Although domesticated pigs are symbolic gifts in the community, pig husbandry has recently been used as a form of monetary exchange within Indigenous communities. Thus, like cattle, pigs can be transferred for both cash value and as a symbol of sacrifice. For instance, one of the Elders said, "The pig does not have cash value in the Bengali market [outside community market] due to mainstream Muslim religious sanctions," thus the pig is mostly used in land and water management spiritual ceremonies.

In summary, the researchers learned that domestic animals have spiritual, relational, and economic values within the community, and can be transformed into symbols of power, inspiration, and support for the community's everyday management practices.

Traditional administrative structure and management

Research participants – particularly Elders, Knowledge-holders, and leaders – agreed that the community's land, water, and forest management were interconnected within the traditional cultivation culture (i.e., the paddy crops, forest resources, cultivation tools, and domestic animals). Participants described management in terms of the relational and spiritual ceremonial function of the domains outlined above. Exemplifying the point, Elder Kosomo Prure Kheyng depicted relationships between agriculture domains and management practices as interconnected "everyday ceremonies."

Although the researchers learned of the community's environmental management through data on agriculture domains, descriptions of traditional administrative structures were also discussed as vital for the community's land, water, and forest practices. Elders and leaders highlighted the Laitu Khyeng geographic location as an important factor in exploring relationships between the community's modes of administrative structure and understanding of management practices. For example, the Chittagong Hill Tracts (CHT) are covered by three Circles,[8] which include the *Bhonong* Circle, the *Chakma* Circle, and the *Mong* Circle. The community's villages are mostly situated within the Bhomong Circle (Adnan, 2004). The traditional administrative structure involves three components: the village, the Mouza (i.e., several villages), and the Circle (i.e., several Mouzas). Within each component, administrative positions are designated (Roy, 2002). The first administrative position is the village manager, known as the *Karbary*; the second administrative position is known as the *Headman*; and the third administrative position is known as the *Raja/King* of the Circle. Each administrative structure has different roles in management, but the three administrative positions are all interconnected. The Indigenous villages have three *Karbary* positions and they work with other Indigenous communities' *Headmen* and *Circle Chiefs* in Mouzas and Circles. The traditional administrative structures control land, water, and forest resource management and distribution in the community. Data on the above three administrative positions are discussed below, illuminating selection criteria (see table 5.1) and responsibilities related to traditional land and water management.

Karbary

At the village level, the *Karbary* administrative position is the most important position related to the traditional Indigenous land, water, and forest resource management structure. The *Karbary* is also known as the village manager and responsibilities include overseeing village forest and plain-land resources and responding to local problems. The village manager can be both selected or elected

Table 5.1 Traditional administrative structure, land, and water management. The traditional administrative structure table is collated from personal and collective stories shared by Elders and community leaders.

Administrative Position Name	Selection Criteria	Responsibilities
Karbary (Village Manager)	• Selected/elected by the village community/ies • Indigenous identity • Special knowledge of village community/ies' customary laws • Special knowledge of village community/ies • Knowledge of spirituality • From own village • Good relationships with village community/ies' members • Decision-making ability	• To be a spokesperson for the village community • To distribute Jhum and plain land among village members • To manage village forest (land and water) • To distribute village forest resources among village members • To act as spiritual leader • To make decisions for the village community
Headman for each Mouza	• Selected/elected mostly through inheritance • Indigenous identity • Respected person • Special knowledge of communities' customary laws	• To distribute forest resources (land and water) among village members • To deal with village *Karbaries'* unsolved problems. • To collect taxes from villages • To work with Circle *Chief* • To work with state forest and Indigenous administrations
Raja/Circle Chief Selected from each Circle (comprising Mouzas)	• Selected mostly through inheritance • Indigenous identity • Respected person • Special knowledge of Indigenous communities' customary laws	• To distribute forest resources (land and water) within *Mouzas* • To deal with village *Headmen's* unsolved problems. • To collect taxes from *Mouzas* • To work with government forest and Indigenous ministries • To work with the other two Circle *Chiefs*

democratically by villagers and is the spokesperson for the village in dealings with *Headmen* and other government administrators.

The village community arranges a sacrifice ceremony to honor a newly selected/elected person. Knowledge-holder Ching Sho Khyeng emphasized that this position cannot be profitable and/or cannot be used for self-interest.

The selection criteria for the *Karbary* position reflects the village community's interests. Following the recommendation of village members, the position is appointed by the Mouza *Headman* for the Mouza area, the Circle *Chief* for the three Circles in CHT area, and the government's Deputy Commissioner (DC). According to customary village law, the *Karbary* position gets selected/elected in the particular interest of village communities. For example, the proposed person must be from the Indigenous community, is required to have special knowledge of the village's customary laws, must have supportive relationships with village communities, must be able to understand and lead spiritual and religious traditions for the village, and must have the ability to make decisions for the village communities to solve local problems. Because the CHT Indigenous administrative structure is maintained by diverse Indigenous communities, being multilingual is another significant quality for selecting a *Karbary*. During the data-collection period, three *Karbaries* were in the Laitu Khyeng Indigenous community (i.e., within our research site). Each *Karbary* was able to speak multiple languages including the community language, the *Marma* language (another Indigenous language), and Bengali (Bangladeshi official language). The qualified candidate's name is proposed to the Mouza *Headman* by community Elders, leaders, Knowledge-holders, and youth leaders. The Mouza *Headman* submits the village members' elected representative to the Circle *Chief*, and the *Chief* relays that representative to the DC for official documentation.

The *Karbaries'* responsibilities for the village include Indigenous land and water management in the community. The village manager is responsible for the control of forest resources and distribution; however, most major decisions take place through a democratic process with village members' consent. During critical times, the *Karbary* promptly calls a meeting that is convenient for participation by all village members. Also, decisions made by the *Karbary* are decided in consultation with the Mouza *Headman*. If there is an important issue or problem regarding cultivation and/or management in the village, the *Karbary* is the first person to try to solve the problem. The *Karbary's* responsibilities can be organized into two broad categories: the first is as land distributor and tax collector, and the second is as spiritual and healing leader. As land distributor and tax collector, one of the main responsibilities of the *Karbary* is to distribute Jhum land among village members. The *Karbary* as spiritual and healing leader represents and leads village spirituality in special cultural and social festivals. The *Karbary* is responsible for arranging ritual programs of sacrifice and dedication to the village ancestors. For these processes, the *Karbary* needs to hold the special knowledge to explain the village's supernatural power[9] (e.g., connection to spiritual realms). Thus, the *Karbary* is the main healer and religious leader as well as the person who directly controls village tax collection, the results of which are then passed on to the Mouza *Headman*.

The *Karbary* is not a paid position; however, the *Karbary* receives gifts from the villagers and a token honorarium from the government. Though the position of *Karbary* is not particularly economically rewarding nor does it offer a significant amount of power, it is a position that offers rich spirituality and allows the individual to contribute to the community's everyday land, water, and environmental management practices.

Headman

According to traditional customary laws, the *Headman* is the administrative head of a Mouza. A Mouza usually encompasses a number of villages with diverse Indigenous communities. The community's traditional land, water, and forest management practices are greatly influenced and/or controlled by the *Headman* who acts as an intermediary between the *Karbaries* and the *Circle Chief* (discussed later). Although the community does not have its own *Headman*, the village *Karbaries* are connected with different Indigenous communities' *Headmen*.[10]

The *Headman* selection categories and responsibilities are different from those of the village *Karbary* administrative position, and the Mouza *Headman* goes through a different selection process. Indigenous identity is the first selection criterion. According to participant Khyeng Elders and Knowledge-holders, their *Headman* is from another Indigenous community and has been selected through an inheritance system. The position has been exclusively inherited by men. In the data, leaders discussed that although the position was mostly selected through heredity, the *Headman* may come from a different community as is the case with the Laitu Khyeng. Such an arrangement is sanctioned on the basis of holding special knowledge about different Indigenous traditional customary laws. According to traditional customary practices, the communities need to respect the *Headman* position whether or not the *Headman* is from a neighboring Indigenous community.

As mentioned, responsibilities of the Mouza *Headman* are different from those of the village *Karbary*. The *Headman* collects taxes from the village *Karbaries* and passes them on to the Circle *Chief*. Aside from collecting taxes, the *Headman* is responsible for addressing any conflicts or problems in the village that the *Karbary* is unable to resolve. The *Headman* is also responsible for distributing forest, land, and water resources among the villages and is tasked with advising the government's District Commissioner (DC) in relation to taxes and other information. The *Headman* distributes community land and forest areas according to customary law and the needs of the community. The community believes that although the traditional administrative *Headman* position is appointed, the selected person must be as neutral as possible in distributing land, water, and forest resources. If the community is not happy with the *Headman's* decisions and/or judgments, they can submit a complaint to the Circle *Chief* asking for justice.

Chief

The *Chief* is the head of the Circle and is known locally as the *Raja* (i.e., King of the Circle). The CHT is overseen by three Circle *Chiefs* who primarily work with the Bangladesh government's Forest, Land, and Indigenous Ministries (Roy, 2000). According to Khyeng Indigenous Elders and Knowledge-holders participating in the study, the three Circle *Chiefs* have direct connections to development agencies (e.g., NGOs, UNDP, UNESCO), tobacco companies, microcredit businesses, and forest management practices but are not associated with policy-making or policy administration (Adnan, 2004). Traditional Indigenous customary laws dictate that the *Chief* is the highest authority presiding over Indigenous communities (Roy, 2000). Although the community does not have a direct connection with the Circle *Chief*, the village *Karbary* and the Mouza *Headman* are responsible to the *Chief*. The Circle *Chief* is responsible for overall forest management within the Circle's Mouzas and villages.

The Circle *Chief* position is primarily inherited and patrilineal, and the position-holder is required to have an Indigenous identity. The Circle *Chief* is a respected position and the holder is expected to be knowledgeable of traditional Indigenous customary laws and practices as well as land-management practices in his Circle.

One of the Circle *Chief's* main responsibilities is to collect taxes from the Mouza *Headmen* and give a substantial portion to the Bangladeshi government. The *Chief* is also tasked with distributing forest, land, and water resources among Indigenous communities. In addition to resource distribution and tax collection, the *Chief* is responsible for resolving the villages' and the Mouzas' unresolved conflicts according to traditional customary laws. The *Chief* has the power to solve problems that cannot be resolved by the initial two levels of leadership. The *Chief*, however, mostly works with the other two Circle *Chiefs* in the CHT.

Traditionally, the Circle *Chief* plays a significant role in protecting Indigenous spiritual and relational land, water, and forest management practices (Adnan, 2004; Chakma, 2010; Roy, 2000). The Elders explained in the data that the Circle *Chief's* responsibilities have changed since the time of their ancestors as a result of interactions with both colonial (British: 1757–1947) and postcolonial state governments (Pakistan: 1947–1971 and Bangladesh: 1971–present). However, Elders still view the Circle *Chief* position with greater esteem than the mainstream state administrators. Elders and Knowledge-holders emphasized in the data that proper knowledge of the Indigenous communities' spiritual ceremonies and everyday management practices is the principal requisite for all three traditional administrative positions (*Karbary*, Mouza *Headman*, and Circle *Chief*).

Spiritual practice and management

Research participants were eager to illuminate why spirituality was an important factor in practicing land, water, and forest management. The researchers were told that the community's everyday management practices with water, land, and forest were interconnected and aligned with their daily spiritual practices. For example, Knowledge-holder Kasamong Prue Khyeng explained the relationship between spirituality and management, stating, "If there is no spirituality, there is no community. Spirituality represents for us taking care of our life and our environment." He explicitly described the connectivity between spirituality and management in the following poem (translated by the Methuei Chaing Khyeng):

> Our spirituality is our Mother Land.
> Our spirituality is our hills, sky, water, and our heart.

Our spirituality always creates our relationships and our knowledge.
Our spirituality created us all in one family.
Our spirituality guides us in how to maintain our relationships with land and water.

Community Elders and leaders explained spirituality in terms of various forms of *puja*: for example, the *Bogle puja* (hilly land/Jhum land spirituality), the *Hanei puja* (water spirituality), the *Lung puja* (stone spirituality), the *Lokhei puja* (cultivation and production spirituality), and the *Soyttobill puja* (production feast festivals). The *puja* is a spiritual prayer or dedication to a supernatural power and/or to ancestors. Research participants believe the *puja* to be sacrifice, love, and relationship. For example, Elder Basa Khyeng explained, "*Puja* is our spiritual power, and it comes from our collective nature gods." The significance of *puja* spiritual practice is connected to the protection of the community and the community's relationship with the environment. The following paragraphs outline participants' views on the relationships between various spiritual practices and the community land, water, and forest management practices.

Bogle puja

As indicated by Elders during sharing circle discussions, the *Bogle puja* was one of the representative spiritualities (mostly celebrated in the Jhum hilly fields). *Bogle puja* is also known as the Jhum god. Elders believe that through the *Bogle puja*, the Khyeng community builds spiritual relationships with Jhum land, animals, plants, and other species. To honor the Mother Forest and increase agricultural production, the Khyeng practice the *Bogle puja* at the Jhum fields and Jhum store. Through performing the *Bogle puja*, the community believes it will be able to produce enough food for the community and will be able to provide adequately for animals. During the *Bogle puja*, the community sacrifices domestic animals to build relationships with Jhum (hilly) land, plants, and wild animals and *Binii dhan* (a special kind of paddy crop mostly used for spiritual purposes). According to Kasamong Prue Khyeng, sowing *Binii dhan* in Jhum land shows respect for the land and acts as a symbol of seeking permission. He added that "the community does not start their Jhum production without seeding *Binii dhan* for the *Bogle puja*."

Hanei puja

Whereas *Bogle puja* is associated with land spirituality, the *Hanei puja* is described as being connected with water spirituality. One of the main purposes of this *puja* is to show respect to the water god for using water in everyday activities. The Khyeng believe that the water god is the source of all water. If the Khyeng community does not take care of its water sources, it may not survive. As indicated by Elder Kosomo Prue Khyeng, they may lose their "Mother-Jhum, Friend-animals, and Brother-waterfalls." Elder Basa Khyeng reinforced this sentiment, describing the

Hanei puja as a ceremony showing respect, honor, and protection for local water resources. The Khyeng celebrate *Hanei puja* during Jhum seeding and Jhum cultivation seasons. Elder Basa Khyeng explained that the Khyeng practice the *Hanei puja* three times during the year: during the New Year celebration, seeding time for Jhum cultivation, and Jhum and plain-land harvest. The community celebrates *Hanei puja* near canals because canals serve as a main source for drinking water and other daily uses. Thus, the canals are revered in association with the *Hanei gods*. In addition to *Hanei puja* celebrations occurring three times a year, the ceremony is also conducted if anyone in the village community becomes seriously ill. During *Hanei puja*, the community sacrifices domestic animals to the water god to bless the community with water and to protect them from illness. The community believes the water god will protect members from sickness and critical health conditions. Leader Ukay Khyeng relayed in the data a prayer to this effect, asking of the water god, "Please protect us from sickness as you give us life."

Youth participant Ukay Khyeng explained that during *Hanei puja* (see Figure 4.3) the Khyeng community restricts access to their village. During these times, no one is permitted to enter or exit the village, and nothing can be brought in from outside nor sent out. If anyone breaks this law, they receive a monetary citation.

Lung puja

The *Lung puja* spiritual celebration is described in the data by Knowledge-holder Ching Shou Khyeng as honoring the significance of big trees within the community. Ching Shou Khyeng explained that traditionally the Khyeng community engaged in this kind of spiritual celebration as a way of celebrating animals, production, trees, and others. A part of celebrating *Lung puja* involves the Khyeng community protecting the big trees in their village. The community celebrates *Lung puja* at the beginning of the New Year. Similarly to Jhum land and water resources, Elder Basa Khyeng explained that big trees play a vital role in the maintenance and protection of community health, crops, and animals and are therefore honored through a spiritual ceremony.

Lokkhi puja

The *Lokkhi puja* is known as a cultivation and harvest spiritual celebration. The *Lokkhi* god is the protector who provides spiritual power toward cultivating land and creating solutions in times of crisis. According to coresearcher participant Nyojy U Khyeng, the *Lokkhi puja* is usually celebrated on Saturday evenings at the top of the hill[11] near the big trees. However, the *Lokkhi puja* can be celebrated every day, and thus each day is considered a spiritual day in the community. During this *puja*, the community sacrifices to the *Lokkhi* god locally produced fruits, flowers, and foods. The villagers pray to the *Lokkhi* god for food sufficiency and for the protection of Jhum and plain land. Elder Basa Khyeng discussed that these acts of sacrifice and dedication were symbols of the harvest spirit in the community.

Soyttobill puja

The *Soyttobill puja* is a feast festival that takes place right after Jhum production as a way of honoring the nature god(s). The *Soyttobill* feast involves preparing a dish that consists of a large variety of harvested foods in a big pot, symbolic of bringing together community members of all ages and genders to share the prepared meal. This act of eating together and sharing is a way of celebrating the foods produced and emphasizes the nature of this *puja* as a symbol of collectiveness. According to Knowledge-holder Kosomo Prue Khyeng, through the *Soyttobill puja*, the Khyeng community believes that all villagers (Elders, youth, and children) can collectively protect their food sources as well as land, water, and animals.

On puja

The *On puja* has an important role in the community's decision-making processes. The community refers to wetland areas as *On* areas, which means that they will not be used for cultivation. In selecting Jhum land in hilly areas, the Khyeng community avoids wetland areas; they believe wetland areas are significant food sources for insects, birds, and animals. The community sees *On* areas, particularly the waterfall areas, as one of the main potable water source for the Indigenous community. Participants discussed in the data that anyone who cultivates *On* areas would reduce the fertility of their land, thereby producing a less ample crop as well as affecting the fertility of the family. Through this and other examples Elder and Knowledge-holder participants expressed that the Khyeng Indigenous community considers their spiritual knowledge to be scientific knowledge.

As stated earlier, the community believes that *On* (i.e., wetland) areas are not of high production quality; however, if anyone wants to cultivate Jhum on *On* land, they need to make sure that there are enough food source areas for the other actors/god(s), such as animals, insects, birds, and others. To use *On* land, the interested person needs to follow a number of rituals such as those indicated in the following scenario from a sharing circle conversation. First, the interested person needs to form a friendship with, and ask permission from, *On*. Second, to obtain permission, the interested person is required to sacrifice a domestic chicken to honor *On* land and have a feast with village members. According to Knowledge-holder Ching Shou Khyeng, the request for permission from *On* is recited as follows: "Oh my friend and brother, please protect me, my children, and my family. Please give us permission to have some food from you. Please forgive me if I do any wrong." Finally, the interested person needs to leave the *On* area if anyone in the family gets sick during cultivation because the community considers sickness a sign that the *On* has not given permission to cultivate the land in question.

In sum, it is clear from community Elders, Knowledge-holders, and leaders that the community's traditional land, water, and forest management (see Figure 4.1) align with their spirituality. Participants emphasized that practicing spiritual and sacrificial ceremonies are connected with Jhum harvest, plain-land cultivation, and water management. The researchers also learned that a good harvest was connected with *puja* and sacrifice rituals and was considered an honor and a sign of a healthy relationship with the land and water gods. Any cultivation practices that dishonor the land and water gods or do not foster healthy relationships with them are considered serious sins and sources of evil spirits. Such sins and emergent evil spirits can invoke the land and water gods to bring unexpected crises, not only to the particular person engaged in cultivation but also to the whole community. Therefore, cultivation practices that honor the gods and maintain healthy relationships with them protect the community from future food crises and illness. Our research team also found from the second sharing circle conversation and individual discussions with Elders and Knowledge-holders that building relationships and honoring supernatural gods are connected with a good harvest. The recipient of a good harvest is supposed to engage in a spiritual ceremony and to share with neighbors by offering a feast. Through these spiritual practices, the Khyeng community believes their environment, identity, and rituals are interconnected with spiritual practices. Therefore, the community prefers to introduce themselves as a spiritual community.

Traditional economy and management

The community's traditional economy was discussed by participants as one of the significant factors in detailing the community's environmental management. During the second sharing circle, Elders and Knowledge-holders explained that the community observed a close relationship between management (everyday cultivation practices) and daily economic activities, such as food production, food exchange, local market transactions, and food preservation. These relationships relied largely, but not entirely, on local input and skills from within the community. According to protocols of the traditional economy, decisions about purchasing various machines and minor equipment needed for economic activities were jointly made with other Indigenous and a few non-Indigenous communities. Data provided by Elders, leaders, and Knowledge-holders are discussed below, highlighting the relationship between the community's economic activities and environmental management.

The community's economic domains[12] are spiritually interconnected with their land, water, and environmental management perceptions. Coresearcher participant Mathui Ching Khyang, depicted in her commonplace book the relationship between economic domains and management as "a flower ring." Drawing from Elders' teachings, she elaborated: "Traditionally our natural resources are our parents who take care of our everyday needs. We as an Indigenous community have grown up with our natural resource blessings."

The community's daily food and nutritional needs are satisfied by their exchange processes. Community members exchange with each other resources such as bamboo shoots, banana stalks, and roots and leaves of various wild plants from forest and woodland. The community also collects various fruits from hilly land and exchanges these in local village markets. In addition to Jhum cultivation, the community grows vegetables, oilseeds, cotton, and turmeric (a cooking spice) in forest/hilly land and sells the produce in the neighboring village. However, transactions within the local village market sometimes involve an exchange of goods or services rather than monetary currency. The forest resources have additional economic value to the community, providing housing and fuel for cooking.

In addition to the cultivation and processing of forest resources, the community economy also depends on wage-based, plain-land crop production. A plow cultivation technique is principally used in plain land to cultivate wet-rice crops, winter vegetables, mustard, chilli peppers, and tobacco. Wage-based labor is also used in the husbandry of grazing cattle. Thus, in addition to the use of forest resources, a proportion of the community's economy is dependent on wage-based employment generated by plain-land cultivation.

The community's fruit crops also play a role in the economy. Some of the community households (those who do not have access to Jhum land due to government reserve forest policies) are dependent on horticulture cash crops such as mango, banana, and orange. However, nongovernmental projects (e.g., Brickfield, tobacco, and profit-oriented wood plants) have created impediments to accessing markets, which have diminished opportunities for cash-crop fruit production.

Raising livestock constitutes another supplement to the community's economic base. Cattle and pigs are the main livestock sources. In particular, pigs have significant economic value because they are not available in mainstream Bengali markets due to the Muslim community's religious restrictions. The Indigenous communities use pigs often for cultural and spiritual festivals. These communities also sell pigs to other Indigenous communities. In addition to spiritual and cultural uses and values, cattle have many other uses in the Khyeng Indigenous community. For example, cow dung is used as an organic fertilizer, and it is sold at the local market as a form of cooking fuel.

In addition to a place of daily spiritual practice and a reservoir for watering crops, local water sources provide an opportunity to fish as well as a place to raise ducks. Fishing is another major supplement to the economy offering employment for both men and women. The community's local water sources consist of two major canals spanning three villages; in these canals, members catch fish for consumption and to sell as a commodity at the local market.

It is evident in the data that traditional economic domains in the community are deeply interconnected with land-water management practices. It is clear from most participants – particularly Elders, Knowledge-holders, and leaders – that the community's explanations of land, water, and management are different from the Western meanings of management. Thus, according to participants, traditional management can be summarized as their everyday relational and spiritual collective practices for themselves and their land, water, and forest resources.

Community meanings of management

As we previously discussed in the findings chapter (theme two), in Western academic discourse the management concept is used in different ways than within an Indigenous worldview (Berkes, 2003, 2009; Nadasdy, 2003). This difference may be illuminated along the following lines: the Western sense of environmental management has been widely criticized as positing humans (particularly Western men) as a superior life form with an inherent right to use and control nature toward individualistic ends (Escobar, 2008; Vos, 2007). Indigenous worldviews, in contrast, see all management entities in a relational context and stress interdependency and justice for all life forms (Lauer & Aswani, 2009). In our study, researchers and participants together identified the Laitu Khyeng community's concept of management in terms of agency, relationality, commonality, and science. Researchers and participants identified the Laitu Khyeng community's concept of management knowledge as practice-based, holistic, and diversity building as well as spiritual and relational.

Practice-based

To the Laitu Khyeng Indigenous community, management practice honors the diversity of everyday life, which includes domestic animals, cultivation tools, types of paddy crops, and forest resources. Such diverse aspects of management represent various agencies in their management practices, each having its own management power in everyday practice. According to the participants, each component has an influence on the community's production, consumption, needs, and time as well as surplus and distribution. Elder Kosomo Prue Khyeng expressed in the data that, "Each animal, plant, and species has its own management power." He also clarified that community members do not believe management is a power that can be used over another; rather, management is comprised from different types of living relationships which have the ability to influence management practices. Similar studies have argued (e.g., Berkes, 2008; Simpson, 2014) that ideas of management practiced within Indigenous communities have diverse meanings and agency.

Holistic

A second management dimension foundational to the Laitu Khyeng Indigenous community involves holistic sharing of power through traditional administrative processes. As an example of this power-sharing practice, the community makes resource management decisions through participatory dialogue among community members. Berkes (2009) discusses power sharing in Indigenous management as a complex process (see also, Nadasdy, 2003). Power sharing can be seen as a move toward equity as in the case of land distribution processes among Indigenous communities in Canada, Australia, Norway, and elsewhere. In the study, we observed that management is enacted through power sharing that is overseen by traditional administrative structures. In this traditional administrative process, everybody owns rights on production and distribution. This aligns with the suggestion of Borrini-Feyerabend et al. (2004) that, "Participatory traditional management needs participatory roots" (p. 175).

Diverse knowledge

Traditional management is discussed in the data as a process of building knowledge diversity among the community. The sharing of traditional knowledge and stories by Elders and Knowledge-holders (about planting, cultivating, fishing, clothing, and spiritual celebrations) is considered a diverse social capital-building process within the community. We (coresearcher participants) noted that the youth who participated in evening story-sharing circles with their Elders built trust as well as acquired diverse knowledge. They learned how to recognize the purpose and behaviors of plants and animals and how to build relationships and care for these plants and animals. Nadasdy (2003) considers diversity in natural resource management a form of social capital. Diversity appears to be a determinant of success across generations in a variety of management processes: a requisite to building and sharing knowledge and fostering effective relationships (Berkes, 2009). For example, Elder Basa Khyeng stated: "Our land, water, forest, animals are our parents. They take care of us and our responsibility is to take care of them. Therefore, we cannot sell them or use them for profit." In addition to a sentiment of responsibility, participants emphasized that the community's management practices have multiple benefits: a) nothing can be owned as an individual commodity and everything belongs to everyone; b) they build relational trust with each other; and c) they construct supportive, respectful, and honorable attitudes among community members. The trust-building processes in environmental resource management allow us to recognize *others* as ourselves (Escobar, 2008; Latour, 2004). In such trust-building arrangements, everything is considered to belong to the community (Adnan, 2004; Escobar, 2008). As Martusewicz (2009) suggested, common practices are helpful "At protecting larger life systems that we need and thus we are actively engaging and protecting collaborative intelligence" (p. 258).

Management as agency

Like other Indigenous understandings of land and water, Laitu Khyeng environmental resource management practices adhere to particular forms of agency: embracing diversity, sharing power, and building trust as part of everyday management practices (Amoamo & Thompson, 2010; Berkes, 2009).

To the Laitu Khyeng Indigenous community, management practice honors the diversity of everyday life, which includes domestic animals, cultivation tools, types of paddy crops, and forest resources. Such diverse aspects of management represent various agencies in their management practices and each has its own management power. According to participants, each component has an influence on the community's production, consumption, needs, time, surplus, and distribution. Elder Kosomo Prue Khyeng expressed in the data that "each animal, plant, and species has owned management power." He also clarified that community members do not believe management is a power that can be used over another; rather, management comprises different kinds of living relationships, which have the ability to influence management practices. Similar studies have argued (e.g., Berkes, 2003; Simpson, 2001) that ideas of management practiced within Indigenous communities have diverse meanings and agency.

In such trust-building arrangements, everything is considered to belong to the community (Adnan, 2004; Escobar, 2008). As Martusewicz (2009) suggested, common practices are helpful "at protecting larger life systems we need and thus we are actively engaging and protecting collaborative intelligence" (p. 258).

Management as a scientific practice

The Laitu Khyeng Indigenous community views their spiritual and relational management practices with the environment as having scientific and ecological significance. The researchers identified examples from participants' discussion, photovoice, and commonplace books in which Laitu Khyeng Indigenous management practices offered solutions to multiple ecological and sociological issues. We discovered that traditional spiritual and relational management can reduce species lost, water crises, logging, weeds, and food crises and that traditional management knowledge increases plant and animal species diversity, women's decision-making power, youth empowerment, organic fertilizers, crop selection, and surplus distribution. Participants also expressed that hybrid, common, and scientific meanings of management practices are essential for reconstructing the Laitu Khyeng Indigenous identity, culture, and sustainable livelihood. Such a narrative can offer the opportunity to reconstruct, communicate, and reclaim Laitu Khyeng traditional Indigenous practices of natural resource management. Berkes (1999), Berkes and Henley (1997), and Berkes and Folke (1998) similarly discussed traditional Indigenous management practices as scientific knowledge. The authors explained that traditional Indigenous knowledge promotes the protection of the remaining components of biodiversity and the unique values of local cultures; in addition, it can enhance the ability of local communities to establish a livelihood. In other words, traditional Indigenous management understandings and practices are considered successful for natural resource management with respect to social, political, economic, and ecological domains (Datta et al., 2014; Wallerstein & Duran, 2006; Walker & Le 2008). Berkes and Henley (1997) also suggested that in seeking practical solutions to environmental and socioeconomic impacts, local Indigenous management knowledge is a vital resource.

Notes

1 According to the Elder Basa Khyeng, the customary laws are their community and other Indigenous communities' ancestral ways of life/rules, which they have been practicing for generations.
2 Different kinds of paddy crops: vegetables, fruit, and other cash crops.
3 Bangladesh forms the largest delta in the world and a large part of its landmass is plains inundated with rivers and tributaries. Small plain lands in valley bottoms, riverbanks, and lower slopes in CHT retain water only during the monsoon. Rice paddies, tobacco, sugarcane, maize, groundnuts, beans, different vegetables, and fruit species are cultivated using plow technology in the plain lands (Adnan, 2004; Roy, 2000).

4 According to Knowledge-holder Kasamo Prue Khyeng the community's *moral value* is based on collective honor toward natural laws (as explained above).
5 Elder Basa Khyeng said, "Our Jhum land is our source of knowledge. Every day we and our children learn many things [relationships, cultivation processes, and responsibilities] from our Jhum land."
6 These include rice, wheat, vegetables, and spices.
7 Participants explained that the community can sell their plain land crops in the local market for cash currency.
8 A Circle is utilized to represent Chittagong Hill Tracts' (CHT) Indigenous communities' geographical designation. A Circle is equivalent to a district (Adnan, 2004). The term is used here for explaining the Laitu Khyeng's traditional administrative structure in relation to their natural resource management practices.
9 According to Elders, a *Karbary* should have proper knowledge of the community's spiritual beliefs, relationships, everyday cultivation practices, and ceremonies (such as harvest, marriage, childbirth, and death).
10 The Laitu Khyeng village Karbaries are responsible to the *Marma* (neighboring Indigenous community) *Headman*.
11 This Top Hill is known as a sacred place to the community. It is situated within the Khyeng villages *Gogro Modrom* and *Gogro Mokh Para*.
12 Elders explained the economic domains such as sufficient food, land, water, and forest resources that are available for each Khyeng family each year.

6 The community's perceptions of current management

> I am very sad, seriously angry, and truly confused as a consequence of the different agencies' [the Bangladeshi government and nongovernmental agencies] artificial, forceful, and discriminative land and water management projects on our motherland.
> – Elder Kosomo Prue Khyeng

> I am a farmer who does not have land to harvest. We lost most of our cultivated land through the government's [Bangladeshi] management projects [lumber and rubber forest plantation, tobacco plantation, Brickfield].
> – Knowledge-holder and school teacher Ching Sho Khyeng

This chapter arose from our research findings and data analysis directly challenging the Western colonial forms of environmental resource management in an Indigenous community; namely, to what extent were the community members affected by introduced land- and forest-management[1] projects, such as those promoted by the government, NGOs, commercial companies, and multinational corporations? Through the research process, the research team endeavored to explore the community's perceptions of the outside agencies' land-, water-, and forest-management projects rather than directly examining the agencies' ideas and policies regarding management. In addition to the use of sharing circles and individual story sharing, data analyzed in response to the question were drawn from photovoice pieces and individual stories shared by youth. Three subthemes emerged from participants' stories: the first centers on the community's perceptions of current management projects (governmental and nongovernmental agencies' land-, water-, and forest-management projects); the second details the projects themselves, contrasting external administrative tenets with traditional Indigenous practices (specifically, the commercial Brickfield industrial company project, the for-profit tobacco plantation project, the wood-plants plantation and reserve forest projects); the third illuminates visible and invisible consequences of the above-mentioned land-management projects, including effects impacting women and species populations. The following section discusses the above three themes and their impacts in relation to community perceptions.

The community's perceptions

This theme emerged from the data illuminating the community's perceptions of the different agencies' (Bangladeshi government and nongovernmental agencies) land, water, and forest resource-management projects within the community. Explaining the community's perceptions of current management practices, participants[2] often told us that rather than contributing to the community's security, the Bangladeshi government and nongovernment agencies' management projects engendered feelings of exploitation, frustration, fear, and danger, thereby posing a formidable challenge for the community.

A sentiment of **exploitation** was frequently conveyed by participants when discussing governmental and nongovernmental land- and forest-management projects in the community. For example, youth leader, activist, and coresearcher Hla Aung Prue Khyeng wrote in his commonplace book that "The current management projects became tools to grab our land." The various agencies' forest- and plain-land-management strategies are perceived by members of his community as mechanisms of exploitation. Similarly, Knowledge-holder Kasamong Prue Khyeng linked non-Indigenous management projects to struggles suffered within the community: "Today we are experiencing food crises and poverty as a result of our government imposing exploitative land and water management projects on our traditional land, water, and forest. All of these current projects are nothing but exploitation to us." Likewise, most other participants pointed out that since forced management projects became commonplace in their community, exploitation also became evident (i.e., lack of access to cultivated lands, food, poverty).

The data revealed that **frustration** was also a common response of community members when reflecting on governmental and nongovernmental management projects. Leader, activist, and coresearcher Kray Prue Khyeng characterized the current management projects as "a root of frustration for us." Two predominant aspects fueling the participants' frustration were: outsiders' power over Indigenous community members and efforts to maximize profits from the community's forest. For example, Knowledge-holder Ching Sho Khyeng stated that the current management projects "are not only hopeless to us but are also seriously oppressive of our Mother Nature."

Current land- and forest-management projects enacted within the community elicit a profound **fear** that spiritual connections and relationships with trees, birds, animals, and plants are being damaged. Coresearcher participant Mathui Ching Khyang depicted the various agencies' management projects as "evil snakes to us [a symbol of fear within the community]." She described the government and development agencies' projects as the "evil snakes" because the "management projects have been intentionally abusing our Mother Nature and displacing us." Elder Kosomo Prue Khyeng reiterated Mathui Ching Khyang's characterization that such projects are a source of fear within the community, stating, "We pass our days in serious fear about nightmare projects on our ancestors' land." Participants stressed that this fear continues to grow as the challenge to maintain the community's traditional management practices becomes increasingly difficult.

Current management projects are also explained by participants in terms of representing a **danger** to the community. For example, one Elder[3] emphasized that the different agencies' management projects are designed "to cut and clear our forest in the name of unproductive land. These projects are dangerous as they are grabbing our motherland to displace us." Participants detailed how the community's forestland and water bodies were transformed into sources of profit for the different agencies' projects. The Knowledge-holders emphasized that most of the projects have created serious challenges for the community's traditional management practices. Coresearcher participant Mathui Khyeng questioned outsider profit-making processes saying

> Who is deciding our practices and management projects for us? Why do they not consider our knowledge of our development projects? Who is responsible for creating poverty in our community? We know our government knew this, but they would not solve it. Our government wants to keep us unprotected through their artificial management projects.

Participants emphasized that management and profit-making were synonymous of outsider management organizations.

It is clear from participants' contributions that the various agencies' conceptions of management diverge from the community's understandings and practices. Taken together, the detrimental impacts of current management projects (exploitation, frustration, fear, and danger) challenge the legitimacy of the projects and the organizations administering them. Participants discussed their objections in terms of settler occupation through which land-grabbing, profit-making, and displacement are achieved. Elder Basa Khyeng explicitly argued that the different agencies' anticommunity management projects have rendered the community essentially unsustainable. Along with Elder Basa Khyeng, additional Elders and leaders outlined how various agencies' management projects contributed to the unsustainability of the community by diminishing the community's ability to provide for itself and lead full lives.

Current (Western) management practices

Theme management practices merged out of the following question raised by coresearcher participants: "Why did the Bangladeshi government and nongovernment land-, water-, and forest-management projects become painful for the community?" In exploring this question, we heard many compelling stories from Elders, Knowledge-holders, leaders, and youth participants. The stories shared by participants are discussed below, illuminating the community's views on particular management projects along with the consequences suffered by the community. The projects most commonly referenced in the data include the following: the government administrative structure, the Brickfield, the tobacco plantations, the for-profit lumber plantations, and the reserve forest projects.

The imposition of the Bangladeshi administrative structure

The imposition of the current state administrative structure on the community's traditional administrative structure was discussed by participants as a form of oppression. One leader explained that although the Chittagong Hill Tracts' (CHT) traditional Indigenous administrative structure started to weaken during British colonial rule, traditional administrative structures have been more aggressively undermined during the Bangladeshi governance period (1971-present). A Knowledge-holder similarly emphasized the impact of the Bangladeshi administration during the 1980s as significantly disempowering the CHT Indigenous community's traditional administrative structure. Evidence of this power grab can also be found in the writings of scholars Adnan (2004), Chakma (2010), and Roy (2000, 2002) who illuminate the oppressive impact of state administrative projects on the CHT community.

A power disparity between the state and traditional Indigenous administrators became evident through discussions with participants. During the first sharing circle, Knowledge-holders expressed that the power disparity between State and Indigenous administrators was created and perpetuated by the Bangladeshi government. One Elder outlined the structural arrangement through which power was unevenly distributed to Bangladeshi administrators.

> According to a hierarchy of administrative power, the CHT Indigenous communities' natural resource areas were divided into five state administrative structures, including: the District Area [i.e., a number of *Thanas*], the *Thana* area [i.e., a number of unions], the *Union* area [i.e., a number of *Mouzas*], the Mouza area [i.e., a number of villages], and the Village area. The position of Circle *Chief* [i.e., the indigenous traditional administrative head] became less powerful in the Bangladeshi state-formed administrative structure during the Bangladesh period (1980s) as the Deputy Commissioner [DC] was converted into the head of the district for judicial and administrative power.

Similar findings disseminated in studies conducted by Adnan (2004), Mohsin (2002), and Roy (2000) confirm that, through the appropriation of control over CHT land, forest, and water resources, the Bangladesh government has diminished the traditional Indigenous administration's power and efficacy to serve the community.

Participants expressed their contention that decision-making power rooted in their ancestors had been taken from the community by state administrators. For instance, one leader outlined how the Bangladeshi government has transferred land-management power from Indigenous leaders to the District Commissioner (DC). He argued that through this process the state administrators' structure became a uniquely powerful authority controlling the community's natural resource and managing processes. As a result of this process, the traditional Indigenous administration became mere tax collectors for the government.

As revealed by participants' stories, the Bangladeshi government's administrative structure presents a significant challenge to the community's traditional natural resource management practices. The community Elders expressed that the state administrators' activities have over time not given importance to the community's traditional administrative structure and traditional management practices. From most participants' perspectives, the imposition of the Bangladeshi state administrative structure over Indigenous administrative structures was characterized as a campaign of force, oppression, and weakening of community stability and self-sufficiency.

Participants described the imposition of state administrators' decision-making processes over Indigenous decision-making as a negative force within the community. For example, one community leader[4] argued that the state administrative structure is a "force to transfer our traditional land and water management decision-making power to the state's administrators." The leader also explained that imposed force by state administrators has negative impacts on the community's traditional management practice. An Elder added, "This force to control our natural resource management rights and decision-making powers is policy-making." Participants frequently argued that state administrative procedure and projects made the Indigenous administration less powerful.

It was clear from conversations with community Elders and Knowledge-holders that the Bangladeshi government, through the state administrators, had helped outsiders[5] to appropriate and control Indigenous communities' natural resources, management rights, and decision-making power. One of the Khyeng schoolteachers described the transformation resulting from state interference as manipulating the community's land and forest resources as "profit-making tools." Therefore, the current imposition of state administrators is considered a serious detriment to the traditional administrative practices and the long-term health and sustainability of the community.

The Brickfield management project

The private Brickfield project was identified in the data as one of the major and most pernicious projects in the community. The community identified it as one of the largest wood-burning brickfield manufacturers within the Bandarban district. Studies (Adnan, 2004; Roy, 2000) also found similar findings that the growing number of brickfields in Laitu Khyeng Indigenous community not only affects mental and physical health but toxic exhaust from production affects crops and plants in adjacent areas. It is one of the major profit-making activities in the community supported by the government administrators. Brickfield production is driven by demand from urban and suburban construction activities as well as road-building projects implemented by the government and private companies (Adnan, 2004). Elders and leaders emphasized that the Brickfield project was a corporate-driven problem, not only in terms of detriment to the community but also in terms of legality, extraction of profits, appropriation of land, and pollution of the environment. The community's views on the project are highlighted below, providing a contextualized representation of participants' perceptions of government interventions in resource management. As Elders emphasized, the Brickfield project has contributed to not only a large loss of cultivated land, plant diversity, and grazing fields, it has also led to a crisis in domestic animals, impacting chickens, ducks, cattle, and pigs.

Notably, Elders depicted the Brickfield industrial enterprise as the most anti-community project on the community's cultivated plain land. Coresearcher Hla Aung Prue Khyeng expressed in his commonplace book that the Brickfield project is a "killing project for our health and our cultivated land." Outlining the community's struggle with the project, the coresearcher stated,

> This Brickfield company took many of our cultivated lands forcefully. We have been fighting to stop this killing project, but the Bangladeshi administration forced us to stop our movement by saying that if we make any movement against this brickfield, the local police authority will put us in jail with fake allegations.

Coresearcher Hla Aung Prue Khyeng also indicated that the Brickfield project significantly reduced the community's decision-making ability, appropriated cultivated land, and created serious unemployment in the community.

During the data-collection process, Brickfield was the largest industrial private company in the community; it was run by an outsider Bengali owner and operated by settler Bengali workers. Community leader and schoolteacher Mongla Pure Khyeng shared his reaction to the Brickfield project: "I feel insane whenever I see this Brickfield on our motherland. Every year hundreds of new settler Bengali workers are coming here." Participants discussed how, through the Brickfield project, outsiders have become more economically and politically powerful in the region, displacing the power of Indigenous people. As an example of the power of the local bureaucracy, Knowledge-holder Kasamo Pure Khyeng explained, "The local court ordered this project to stop, but the local government administrators have been giving support for its continuation." Lamenting these circumstances, the Knowledge-holder was very upset and sadly explained, "Outsiders come to our community to make a profit and leave our forest and our relationships in danger." Participants explained that there are thousands of Brickfield workers coming from outside the Chittagong Hill Tracts (CHT). Most of them do not have any knowledge of Indigenous cultivation culture, rituals, and traditions. Knowledge-holder Ching Shao Khyeng detailed the significant consequence of this land appropriation in the following statement:

> Sixty percent of our community plain-land food sources were coming from the Brickfield area prior to the Brickfield company becoming established. We used to cultivate paddy crops, vegetables, and fish in this area. Most of us did not have food crises in our families. Now we have lost both our land and our forest to this project and we cannot use our water as it is polluted as a result of being used in the brickfield.

An Elder participant also explained that the owner of the Brickfield forcibly bought Indigenous people's land and also used Bangladeshi administrative power over the community to force the sale of the cultivated land.

The youth participants in this book study perceived the Brickfield as a persistent curse imposed upon the community. The youth participants explained their most recent community youth movement against the Brickfield, an action that was covered in the national news media.[6] In this news coverage, the national reporter asked the Bangladeshi administrator when the illegal Brickfield industrial company would cease operation. According to the report, although the Bangladeshi government administrator acknowledged that the Brickfield company was started without community consent, the government administration did not promise to take any initiatives to stop this project.

The Brickfield project has led to significant poverty within the community. The research team observed that the community's livestock grazing areas have significantly diminished because of the development of the Brickfield. One account of this loss, provided by schoolteacher Mongla Prue Khyeng, highlighted the decline of domestic animals, such as cattle, pigs, sheep, ducks, and chickens. Reinforcing the point, Elder Okko stated, "The Brickfield in our village created serious poverty in the community; 60% of our people lost their cultivated land to this project." Knowledge-holder and schoolteacher Ching Chau Khyeng explained how the Bangladeshi government administration has violated the Bangladesh forest laws by giving permission to outsiders to develop this project. He illuminated that according to the Bangladesh Forest Department Policy (BFDP):

> The Brickfield industrial company cannot be built within five kilometers of forested areas, but our village's Brickfield industrial company is within half a kilometer of forest area.

Similarly, youth leader, president of Khyeng Student Council, and co-researcher participant Hla Prue Khyeng explained in his commonplace book that local administrators violated the country's education and cultivation laws by issuing a license to the Brickfield company – owned and operated by outsiders – though the industrial site is located within 5 meters of a primary school and 50 meters of cultivated land.

Participants outlined details of how the Brickfield industry introduced harmful pollutants into the community, strongly condemning this outcome. For example, Knowledge-holder Kasamong Prue Khyeng said:

> The Brickfield project has been creating high levels of carbon monoxide, fluoride, and sulphur in our community. We have been experiencing serious diseases over the last ten years as a result of this project, which we had never experienced before. As you know, just yesterday, one young boy died [during our field visit, February – June 2013] from an unknown disease. Now my wife has cancer.

Building on this, Elders expressed that, due to the close proximity of the Brickfield to the school, many children have experienced breathing problems and, according to Knowledge-holder Ching Shao Khyeng, have contracted "other diseases that we did not know before." Notably, coresearcher Hla Aung Prue Khyeng expressed that "Many parents believe this project causes severe pneumonia and meningitis among the children. Since we [community people] do not have another school within five to six kilometers, villagers do not have a choice."

In summary, it is apparent from participants' discussions that the Brickfield industrial company negatively impacts the community in a multitude of ways, including reduced fertility of the plain land, polluted sources of drinking water, increased deforestation, and possible consequences related to child health. The data also revealed that the project has become a major cause of new settlement in the community.

Profit-oriented forest management

The Bangladeshi government's second-largest management project discussed by participants involves a series of for-profit lumber plantations (i.e., planted trees in place of the natural forest), driven by government forest-management agendas (see Figure 6.1). During the third sharing circle, the majority of participants indicated that the profit-driven plantations are not only detrimental to the community's environment but also seriously impact the community's food sovereignty and spiritual practice. Historically, two forest-management projects, owned by both

Figure 6.1 Profitable plantation project over natural forest. This photo is from Hla Aung Prue Khyeng (coresearcher participant). The top part of the picture indicates a profitable commercial plantation, and the bottom part of the picture shows natural forest. This picture is representative of many hills in the community.

government and private companies, have significantly impacted the community. The first project is a government timber plantation known as the Reserve Forest (RF), which also involves arrangements with illegal logging companies. The second project is run by the Bangladesh Forest Industries Development Corporation (BFIDC), a private corporation designed to make a profit by replacing natural forestation with commercial forests. Participants' views on these two projects and their negative impacts on the community are discussed below.

The government RF is the major forest-management project located within the community. An Elder explained that a large area of traditional forestland was designated as RF during the postcolonial period by the successive states of Pakistan (1947–1971) and Bangladesh (1972–present). Knowledge-holder Ching Shao Khyeng illuminated that, according to legislation around Bangladesh RF, the local community does not have access to their ancestors' land. Community leader and activist Nyojy U Khyeng explained how the RF developed in the Laitu Indigenous community: "We had 3000 hectares of land which was known as the Khyeng complex. This large amount of land [was] declared to be RF by post-colonial state governments [i.e., Pakistan and Bangladesh]." The RF enables illegal logging for non-Indigenous outsiders through forest department administrative support. Coresearcher participant and youth leader Mathui Ching Khyang explained in her commonplace book how the government RF project changed her community's economic balance. She wrote, "The RF is not only a mechanism for taking our forest from us; it has also become a place for illegal logging and fuel wood supply for the Brickfield." Elders and leaders explained that illegal logging has increased within the RF due to the political power acquired by illegal logging interests in relation to the Bangladesh forest department. A leader argued that, "In most cases, the logging companies' owners have connections with local police and the forest department. For this reason, community members cannot do anything."

The second major forest management project in the community discussed by participants is operated by the BFIDC. The project's main objective is to make a profit by planting cash-crop lumber plantations within areas in which natural forest has been clear-cut. Elders explained that the BFIDC is a privately owned company and most of its Bangali owners are from an external, non-Indigenous community. According to the coresearcher participants, three of these owners command more than 60% of profitable lumber plants in the community's forestland. Elders and Knowledge-holders explained that the Bangladeshi government administrators support the outsiders in their grab of the community's forest land. One Elder said that "The outsider owners are politically powerful; they forcibly occupy most of our forest resources and Jhum lands. They cleared our natural forest area and planted profitable *segun* [*Tectona grardis* – teak]."

The for-profit plantation project was introduced primarily to appropriate Indigenous land in order to generate profits for outside interests. An Elder explained that the plantation owners and supporters acted as direct participants in the forced seizure of the community's forest and cultivated land enclosed within the project. For instance, a community Knowledge-holder explained

> We had hundreds of hilly mountains. We used to cultivate *Jhum* on these lands and we did not have a food crisis in our community. The outsider Bangali

people came to our land and took ownership of our motherland through our lack of knowledge of Bangladesh land laws. The Bangali administrators are not interested in understanding the Indigenous peoples' relationships with our mother forestland.

Building on this, Knowledge-holder Ching Sho Khyeng detailed how Bangali-owned lumber plantations have destroyed traditional food cultivation systems. He stated, "In my village the for-profit plantations, on our traditional forest land, destroy our traditional crops such as paddy, banana, maize, sesame, cotton, potato, and pumpkin."

The BFIDC and RF agencies have prioritized profitable wood plantations over the traditional Indigenous forest plants and Jhum cultivation. The new profit-driven plantations in the community include species such as: segun (*Tectona grardis* – Teak), rubber (*Hevea brasiliensis*), and gamari (*Gmelina arborea*). Such forest-management projects are known to the government as green plantations and typically grow woody tree species. According to Elder Kosomo Pure Khyeng, the government forest department and private companies cut down the forest to create new timber plantations for future state economic holdings without community consent. He further argued that monoculture plantations, initiated by the Bangladeshi government forest department, have destroyed the community's traditional and spiritual forest.[7] The Elder further explained that it is an "artificial forest" plantation project that has only created "monocultures of exotic species and destroyed our mother forest biodiversity." Coresearcher Mathui Ching Khyang wrote in her commonplace book that "The BFIDC does not have space for traditional animals, birds, and plant diversity. It produces only one particular profitable wood plant [segun]." The community's species diversity has been significantly reduced as a result of the BFIDC, the government RF, and the illegal logging companies. Elder Kosomo Prue Khyeng stated that many traditional plants, animals, and birds are becoming extinct due to the projects. Elder Kosomo Prue Khyeng emphasized that all of the agencies "use clear-filling [cleaning natural forest and growing profitable plantations] methods in community forest." Elder Basa Khyeng added that more than 100 plant species were removed from the community's forest areas at the hands of the BFIDC, RF, and the illegal logging companies. Clearing natural forest in order to plant commercial crops has also led to serious soil erosion in the forested land.

Current forest management projects (both RF and BFIDC) have had serious repercussions for the community's drinking-water sources. Knowledge-holder Kosomo Prue Khyeng detailed how the for-profit woody trees project created a negative impact on the community's drinking water.

> I can remember, in 1992–1995, we used to get our drinking water if we could dig 1–2 meters of soil. Now, because of the lumber plantation project, we need to dig 200 to 300 meters of soil for drinking water. Since digging for water became expensive, we have been facing difficulties for drinking water and cultivation. Now, we need to walk 1–2 kilometers for drinking water and need to wait for rain to cultivate.

Elders, Knowledge-holders, and leaders concurred that poverty became widespread within the community as a result of the government RF and private BFIDC management projects. One Elder stated, "Both government and private owners do not care for our natural forest, animals, and diversity. They just see our mother forest as a profit-making place." He further explained how the different agencies created poverty in their community: "We used to get all of our food from our forests and did not need to go to outside markets for anything. Now, due to this artificial forest management, we cannot cultivate our food and do not get animals for hunting."

It is evident from the data that participants are united in their condemnation of non-Indigenous forest management projects: the BFIDC, the government RF, and the illegal logging, imposed upon their community. Principles of traditional management and natural forest diversity have been ignored by both the BFIDC and the government RF agencies. The projects have not only undermined Indigenous traditional land-management practices; they have also created a number of negative impacts, such as loss of Indigenous land, obliteration of natural forest diversity, food and water crises in the community, and destruction of relational and spiritual places.

The tobacco plantation and management

The production of tobacco was discussed by participants as the third-largest cash crop introduced into the community. A number of national and multinational companies have established operations within the community, including the British American Tobacco Company, Abul Tobacco Company, and Virginia Tobacco Company. Elders explained that the national and multinational tobacco companies have forcibly taken over the community's fertile plain land to produce tobacco for export. Participants explained that most of the tobacco companies played an active role in not only destroying the fertile cultivated land but in also expanding disease and deforestation in the community.

Participants illuminated that tobacco cultivation began in the community through a series of oppressive strategies. Knowledge-holder Ching Sho Khyeng explained that as a result of families being forced to produce tobacco on their cultivated land, they have become dependent on the market for their daily provisions. The Knowledge-holder claimed that more than 30–40% of Khyeng families became impoverished as a result of the tobacco project. Community Elder Basa Khyeng characterized the introduction of tobacco within the community as a condition of "serious exploitation." He stated, "This project has been creating 'a hole' in our community" through a loan business[8] so that "we cannot come out from under this oppressive process." During the data-gathering process, participants reported having to take loans in cash and in kind from traders and moneylenders who exploited them by imposing onerous terms and conditions on loan payments.

Elder Okko Khyeng explained that tobacco plantations, as profit-making enterprises, represent "a serious danger for us." He elaborated on this danger, stating that the tobacco plantations are "damaging our health, spiritual practices with our land, food sufficiency, domestic animals, and soil fertility." Similarly, coresearcher participant Hla Kray Prue Khayang referred to tobacco cultivation as a "serious health danger," and, although "most of the villagers did not know its negative impacts at first, now, we are experiencing serious negative health and environmental impacts on our community villagers after five years of a tobacco plantation." The Khyeng schoolteacher Mongla Prue Khyeng revealed that the tobacco companies routinely use children as a form of cheap labor. Confirming this, Knowledge-holder Kasamong Pure Khyeng described worker demographics witnessed at a typical tobacco operation: "If you go to every tobacco plant field and burning house, you will see most of the workers are our children. They are working along with their parents all day long." He added sadly, "You will find many family members have been suffering serious unknown diseases. We do not know these diseases' names; we never experienced them before."

The tobacco plantations have also caused serious **deforestation** of the community's forestland. The three villages have eight tobacco leaf burning houses, and these burning houses continuously use forest wood for burning several tons of tobacco leaves in a span of four to five months each year (mostly during the spring). According to Elder Basa Khyeng, "Each day one tobacco burning house needs more than 100 kilograms of firewood, and this turns into almost a ton per day for eight burning houses." Elder Kosomo Prue Khyeng explained that all of the firewood comes from the local community's forest. In most cases, he emphasized, the tobacco companies use this large amount of firewood without informing the Bangladesh Forest Department. However, the tobacco companies have the tacit support of local administrators. Female leader, activist, and coresearcher Hla Kray Prue Khayang, provided an estimate in her commonplace book regarding the link between the tobacco companies' firewood supply and deforestation.

> Each month one burning house uses almost three to five tons of forest wood, and in a season one burning house uses 18 to 25 tons of forest wood. On average, the 8 burning houses use 150 tons of firewood from three Laitu villages. This large amount of firewood comes from our forest resource, in most cases by illegal logging.

According to Elder and *Karbary*[9] Kosomo Prue Khyeng, tobacco plantations in the community have created serious poverty as a result of their destructive practices. He explained how community members got involved with the tobacco plantation projects and became impoverished as a result: "Most of the families obtained loans in a crisis and/or sometimes tobacco companies have given loans forcefully with high interest." According to Elder Okko Khyeng, most of the companies started giving loans under the pretext that, "You will not get loans in a crisis if you do not take loans now." In most cases, families were then unable to pay back their high-interest loans through limited Jhum cultivation. Coresearcher participants explained that private tobacco company loans have a high interest rate, in most cases 30–40%. Thus, most families (those who borrowed during the crisis) struggle to rise above debt linked to tobacco cultivation. Most of the villagers who obtained loans from the tobacco companies are now forced to grow tobacco on cultivated land previously designated for producing sustenance for the family and community.

In addition to adverse effects on the economic and agricultural security of the community, the tobacco companies create a great risk to the community's health, particularly impacting the health of the community's children. As related in participant observations, children are working in tobacco plant fields and tobacco burning houses. Elder Basa Khyeng illuminated how health was further integrated with Khyeng families' reliance on credit issued by tobacco companies. He explained, "If we need to find out our diseases and take medication, again we need to borrow money from tobacco companies. We do not have a choice; we are in a hole now."

Elaborating further the effects on community health and food security, participants explained that the tobacco plantations decline plain-land fertility and contaminate the community's water sources. Tobacco farmer and Knowledge-holder Kasamong Prue Khyeng explained that contamination derives from tobacco farmers' need to use high quantities of chemical fertilizer three to four times a year and, in his assessment, "This strong chemical highly reduces our plain-land soil fertility." Likewise, a second tobacco farmer and Elder stated, "If the land is used once for tobacco cultivation, we cannot use it again for our food production within the next three years." The Elder also indicated that many community members cannot use the local water source due to high levels of contamination. Elder Basa Khyeng confirmed the restricted use of water resulting from tobacco field contamination.

> We used to use our local water source for our everyday needs before the tobacco plantation project on our land. Now we cannot use our local canal water source near the tobacco plant area. We need to go to other villages for everyday water.

In summation, participants explained that the community is at the margin of the poverty line as a consequence of the tobacco project. Coresearcher participant Hla Prue Khyeng wrote in his commonplace book that the tobacco project has "on one hand destroyed our cultivated land and our health and, on the other hand, demolished our forest resources." Similarly, Elder Okko Khyeng asserted that, "The state administrators are responsible for this anticommunity tobacco plantation project on our land and its outcomes."

While most participants connected current management projects to visible negative impacts imposed upon the community, some appeared to also privilege the benefits associated from such projects. One of the Elders[10] said, "In our community there are some Indigenous people who have benefited from the government and nongovernment projects to escape from their poverty. You will find some Indigenous people who are in favor of the government projects." Offering a possible qualifier to this statement, a Knowledge-holder explained why some of the Indigenous people promote anticommunity projects by stating

> During poverty or sickness those [Indigenous] who took out a loan and got benefits from various project owners [e.g., tobacco, Brickfield] were not able to return it. These Indigenous people [those who took a loan from companies] have to talk in favor of anticommunity projects; otherwise, they have to pay back their debt.

Using examples from participant conversations, the researcher team learned that the current land, water, and forest management projects (both governmental and nongovernmental agencies) were far different from the community's traditional management practices. Most of the participants claimed that the current management practices have created not only the above-discussed visible negative impacts but also invisible impacts on the community's everyday life.

The invisible negative impacts

Thus far, we have discussed negative impacts created by the Bangladeshi government and nongovernment land- and water-management projects. Although some of the less visible negative impacts overlap with the visible, we were advised by Elders and Knowledge-holders to include an additional section in order to discuss additional themes from the data. In particular, negative impacts discussed by participants centered around the effect on women in the community and on traditional forest species: for example, forced migration and traditional species extraction. In this subtheme, the Elders and Knowledge-holders re-emphasized women's disempowerment, invisible displacement, and losing traditional species diversity.

Women's disempowerment

As illuminated by most female participants, stories addressing the disempowerment of women, resulting from the various agencies' land, water, and forest management projects are among the most compelling and painful. According to female Elder Shoi Khyeng, the privately owned Brickfield project is a major barrier to women's participation in traditional cultivation practices and educational opportunities. The Brickfield industrial company has undermined the community's traditional collective work environment. Coresearcher Hla Kray Prue Khyeng explained that traditionally the Khyeng used to work together (i.e., all genders and ages) from early morning to evening; however, this collective working environment recently changed with the introduction of the Brickfield private industrial company. This coresearcher participant also explained how the Brickfield industrial area became threatening due to a large number of male settler laborers. Since Brickfield is situated between three villages, the community women cannot go to work or to other villages without passing the Brickfield area. Female Elder Shoi Khyeng explained that many of the women reported having uncomfortable experiences with the male laborers. Hla Kray Prue Khyeng further detailed the danger posed by the Brickfield workers: "Community people fear outsiders [non-Indigenous laborers] often sexually assault our women even in daytime. They [the Bangali settler Brickfield workers] are a big group; we cannot protest". Another coresearcher participant, Mathui Ching Khyang, explained how the workplace has become constricted for females in the community: "I am seriously angry about this Brickfield. I cannot do anything but cry. It [Brickfield] grabbed our working space and freedom." A large number of Bangali settlers became a barrier to the community's traditional practices. "We have to keep silent or stop going to work for them. We are scared to go to our Jhum and plain land." Coresearcher participant Mathui Ching Khyang emphasized further how the Brickfield become a source of fear for her.

> Every day when we pass this area, we feel seriously scared. We are scared of Bangali workers touching us while we are passing this area. We are afraid and ask ourselves, "Will we be able to return to our home safely?" When we think of this Brickfield, we cannot sleep silently at night.

During our fieldwork, we witnessed lots of community women who did not feel comfortable passing the Brickfield area to get to the forest area for Jhum cultivation work.

Invisible displacement

Participants explained that the Bangladesh land-management projects are indirectly forcing Khyeng women to migrate to cities to perform cheap garment labor. A Knowledge-holder participant – father of garment workers – cried and shared painful stories of the reasons he had to send his daughters to secure garment-production work. The participant explained, "Since our Jhum land and plain cultivated lands became limited by the government land and water projects [e.g., Brickfield, lumber plantation, tobacco plantation, and RF], we do not have a choice; we have to send our children for garment work in the city." This Knowledge-holder participant was continuously crying and asked

> Who wants to send their children for garment work? They [the Brickfield, the Reserve Forest, and the tobacco companies] grabbed our ancestors' land. We do not have land to cultivate. I cannot feed my family. I did not have a choice without sending them for low-paid jobs.

He further explained that, even though garment factory labor is low paying, exploitative, and abusive, due to the village's limited forest resources the family was forced to send their children to work in a garment factory:

> We cannot see our daughters for a long time; they cannot afford to come to see us. Our daughters are working 12–18 hours a day but get 70 Taka[11] [less

than a dollar per day]. They cannot even eat properly; they mostly do not have weekends and holidays and live with 20 other workers with limited bathroom and cooking facilities. We also cannot feed them; they want to come back, but we do not have work in the village.

The Knowledge-holder related the view of her daughters,[12] exemplifying the process of indirectly forced migration through sharing her migration story.

> It is very painful to sit at home with very limited work and food. Though we do not want to go for low-paid garment work as we do not feel empowered as we have before in our village community, we do not have a choice. We need to feed ourselves at least.

It is apparent from most of the women participants that current land and forest projects have created serious negative consequences for women, including impacts on women's decision-making ability, working space, freedom of movement, and access to cultivated land.

The community, like other Indigenous communities in the Chittagong Hill Tracts (CHT), used to be a community that empowered women. According to community Elders and Knowledge-holders, the Khyeng community women used to make decisions for self, children, family, production, cultivation, and so on. However, the decision-making capabilities of women have significantly changed recently (e.g., over the last twenty years). Participants explained that reduced Jhum production due to the RF and for-profit plantation has negatively influenced the community's traditional practices, in particular, women's decision-making power and workplace freedom. An Elder described a childhood memory, highlighting that the opportunities she had as a youth cannot be provided to their daughter.

> I remember when I was a child; we had lots of land and most of the land we did not need to cultivate. We did not even need to work every day. We used to dance every evening after work. Our parents used to work and make decisions together. They both used to go to the market and cook for everyone – together.

Coresearcher participant Hla Kray Prue Khyeng discussed the threats to this empowerment resulting from the Bangladeshi government's land and water management projects. A female garment worker explained how the government management projects seriously undermined traditional management practices and created food crises in her family and community. Another coresearcher participant Mathui Ching Khyang said, "I do not see gender inequality in the community. However, since I cannot go to work and market like before, I feel alienated and cannot decide anything from home. Sometimes I get angry that I was born at this time." Furthermore, "Since most of the families do not have enough cultivated land and/or cannot go to work, they have been facing food crises for the last ten years."

Loss of traditional species diversity

Elders and Knowledge-holders explained that species loss has had a serious negative impact on the community. Participants explained that the current management projects – the Bangladesh Forest Industries Development Corporation (BFIDC) and Government Reserve Forest (RF) – appropriated Jhum land from the forest, which resulted in high rates of species extinction. Participants asserted that the socioecological impacts of the projects include: increased labor inputs (e.g. weeding) in both Jhum and plain-land cultivation; altered crop selection in both Jhum and plain-land cultivation; interruption of optimal cycles of cultivation periods (traditionally, Jhum land is cultivated every three years; the loss of land has necessitated a shorter cycle); and increased food crises in the community.

The pressure of government land- and water-management projects adversely affects the productivity of Jhum and wild production. According to Knowledge-holder Kosomo Prue Khyeng, the reduction of forestland due to RF and BFIDC encroachment has significantly impacted ecosystem diversity. The Knowledge-holder explained that roughly 200–300 species of trees have become extinct. During a fieldwork component of the study, the research team[13] also found a difference in heterogeneity among large plants grown on natural hilly land and for-profit plantation land. Vegetation heterogeneity was 85% in hilly Jhum land and only 3% in land used for cash-crop agriculture. We also found a difference in vegetation heterogeneity among the Jhum territories. On the Jhum lands near a government for-profit plantation, vegetation heterogeneity was 65%, as compared to the Jhum lands one kilometer away from the government plantation where vegetation heterogeneity was 95%. In addition, Elder Okko Prue Khyeng said that they experienced large numbers of weeds in Jhum lands close to for-profit plantations. The Elder detailed the difference in productivity between traditional crops grown adjacent to for-profit plantations and those grown in locations far removed from the plantations: "We get an average of 30–40 *Hari*[14] rice in one hector of Jhum land which is near for-profit forest, and we get 60–80 *Hari* rice from our deep forest which is one kilometer away from for-profit forest."

It is clear from the participants' discussion that the various agencies' for-profit land and forest management projects introduced within the community are directly connected with the disempowerment of women and the expansion of species extinction from plain-land and forest resources. It was clear in the data provided by Elders and Knowledge-holders that these processes are directly related to the poverty, food crisis, and unemployment endemic within the community.

Forms of neocolonialism

In this chapter we can see how current governmental and nongovernmental management practices (i.e., Western) enacted within the Laitu Khyeng community have been revealed as the means through which poverty, health problems, land appropriation, and environmental degradation have become endemic in the region.

Another main issue revealed in the findings involves the impacts of contemporary agencies' (both government and nongovernmental) colonial natural resource management policies on the Laitu Khyeng Indigenous community's diverse and relational understanding and practices of land and water management. As outlined in chapter 2, the CHT were colonized by Britain (1757–1947), Pakistan (1947–1971), and Bangladesh (1971–present). Although Bangladesh achieved independence from Britain (1947) and Pakistan (1971), the impacts of colonialism on the CHT and the Laitu Khyeng Indigenous community persist. This book's study's findings reveal three major impacts that can be attributed to the effects of colonialism: the privileging of non-Indigenous natural resource management knowledge over Indigenous knowledge, of the state's administrative structure over Indigenous structure, and of outsider, profit-oriented development projects over Indigenous land and forests.

The consequence of valuing non-Indigenous knowledge over Indigenous knowledge was discussed as a significant colonial impact on the Laitu Khyeng Indigenous community's traditional natural management practices. Participants argued that Indigenous understandings and practices were significantly undermined by outsiders' (governmental and nongovernmental) land policies and projects. For example, Elder Basa Khyeng stated that the different governmental and nongovernmental agencies' management practices were characterized as indisputably profit-driven, detached, and certain of their method. Adnan (2004) drew similar conclusions, stating that in the CHT the Laitu Khyeng Indigenous people were "clearly exploited and dominated by Bengali [non-Indigenous people] while also being neglected by government and agencies of the state" (p. 72). Indigenous scholars Tuck (2012) from North America and Chakma (2010) from South Asia showed how a settler colonial framework privileges settler knowledge over Indigenous knowledge. Other researchers have argued (Berkes, 2003, 2009; Escobar, 2008; Roy, 2000) that outsider management practices on Indigenous land can be a significant barrier to Indigenous sustainable practice due to both the consideration of land as profitable, static, and exploitable and to processes disembodying social life from local connections.

Non-Indigenous environmental management knowledge can lead to dangerous consequences for the local environment. For example, participant Elders, Knowledge-holders, and leaders expressed that the modern management policies have not only eroded traditional Indigenous environmental management knowledge but have also led to species extinction, illegal logging, deforestation, soil degradation, illegal migration, land appropriation, and poverty in the community. Elder Basa Khyang said that the imposition of the state's natural resource management practices over Indigenous practices emerged as a unilateral perspective of management and represented a serious threat to the community. Theorists have similarly argued (Berkes, 2003; Bowers, 2006; Escobar, 2008; Martusewicz, 2009; Smith, 2008; Spivak, 2006; Shiva, 2005) that outsiders' management practices undermine and obstruct traditional communal practices through different development projects.

The Bangladesh non-Indigenous administrative structure is also identified as a significant colonial influence on the Laitu Khyeng Indigenous community's natural resource management. Participants explained that the state administration took control over Indigenous land, water, and forest rights away from traditional Indigenous administrative entities. Adnan and Dastidar (2011) commented that the Bangladeshi state administration was advanced over the Indigenous structure based on the pursuit of profits (p. 124). The authors argued (see also Adnan, 2004; Chakma, 2010) that state administrative structures in the CHT were connected with "various kinds of fraudulent activities and forgeries" (p. 124). Adnan and Dastidar (2011) further emphasized that "the Forest Department has had a land-devouring role to date, grabbing Pahari [Indigenous] lands and promoting commercial plantations through aid-funded projects, while destroying the last of the natural forests of the CHT" (p. 125). Similar conclusions were arrived at in studies conducted by CHT Indigenous scholar Chakma (2010) and Roy (2000).

Participants commented that the privileging of state administration over traditional Indigenous administration has led to the growth of unwanted development projects, projects that benefit neither local communities nor the local environment. Consistent with data provided by study participants, Adnan (2004) indicated that Khyeng community members "reported that they received little protection or help from the local police, administration, and government officers. The officials and functionaries of these institutions were predominantly Bengali" (p. 71).

Outsider, for-profit management projects are highlighted in the data as a form of colonial oppression imposed upon the Khyeng Indigenous community. Participants emphasized the role of for-profit companies in contributing to the exploitation, displacement, deforestation, species extinction, and poverty that has devastated the community. The term outsider, used to depict invasive for-profit companies, may be clarified through drawing on Edward Said's (1993) seminal work *Orientalism*. Said claimed that the imposition of the colonial outsider over local populations requires an unequal system of force leading to processes of *otherness*. According to Said, the outsider creates forms of oppression and power inequality imposed upon local people, much like the relationship between the occident and the orient and the hegemonic nature of colonial power. Escobar (2008) gave an in-depth explanation of how capital accumulation in globalized monoculture environmental resource management not only creates profit for owners but also removes local people, their traditional practice, and their identity. Study participants emphasized that the various entities imposing monoculture and for-profit management projects and policies onto the Laitu Khyeng community have created marginalization or *othering* on their ancestors' land.

In sum, the introduction of resource management policies and projects in the Laitu Khyeng community are a mechanism of ongoing colonialism in the region. Participants repeatedly argued that it is oppressive to change Indigenous cultures for the benefit of outsider resource extraction. In order to get to the root of the Laitu Khyeng Indigenous colonial problem in CHT, it is necessary to understand that colonial oppression is ongoing and is enacted via non-Indigenous, outsider profit-makers, state administrators, and unwanted management projects.

Notes

1 According to Elder and Knowledge-holder participants, management is discerned from four governmental and nongovernmental projects underway in the community: reserve forest, tobacco plantation, lumber plantation, and Brickfield industrial company. We use the term *project* for exploring management policies associated with these projects throughout the data.
2 In some parts of this chapter we have included participants' information, and in some parts we have not disclosed participants' information in accordance with their request.
3 Due to the politically sensitive nature of speaking about government and nongovernment management projects, some participants wished to remain anonymous in the dissemination of data on the topic.
4 As with the political sensitivity perceived in discussing current governmental and nongovernmental management projects, some participants preferred to remain anonymous when speaking about government and nongovernmental agencies themselves.
5 According to Elders and Knowledge-holders, the word *outsider* refers to nonindigenous Bengali: those who don't live in the community. In other words, this encompasses Bangladeshi State administrators who are mostly from outside the CHT (Adnan, 2004).
6 Retrieved March 11, 2018, (Prothom alo: Dec, 26, 2013) www.prothom-alo.com/bangladesh/article/108448/.
7 According to Elders, the community has a spiritual connection with the forest. The forest is considered a god who provides cultivation space, drinking water, and a spiritual space for everyone.
8 Nongovernmental microcredit business in the community (Adnan, 2004).
9 Village leader.
10 A request for anonymity by some participants also extended to statements made involving members of the community.
11 The name of Bangladeshi currency.
12 Participants who work in the garment factories requested that the research team protect their anonymity to avoid reprisal from factory management.
13 We (coresearcher participants and I) surveyed in two different random quadrants (1x1m) with a 50-meter radius around the point count station to conduct a detailed assessment of vegetation and habitat at the site. Each habitat was at least 100m apart from the other habitats. Global positioning system (GPS) location and elevation were recorded for each point. Three features were measured at each habitat: shrub land area, total vegetation cover, and vegetation heterogeneity (percentage cover of three major aquatic vegetation life forms, land form elevation, slope, disturbance indicators, plant community). Vegetative heterogeneity was evaluated for each habitat using the Shannon-Wiener Diversity Index (Gray, 2000), using the percentage cover of each vegetative group as abundance data.
14 One *Hari* equals 10 kilograms. Hari refers as 10-kilogram basket.

7 The community's perceptions of environmental sustainability

In this chapter, we are interested in exploring how an Indigenous understanding of sustainability can inform educational reform in the country. In this chapter, we present a range of learning experiences, drawing on everyday practices that collectively establish the kind of capacity we see as potentially creating the conditions to explore the meanings of sustainability in environmental education. To explore the meanings of sustainability in environmental resource management from the perspective of Indigenous communities where diverse concepts such as relationality, hopes, dreams, expectations, and imagination interconnect, we as researchers need to first acknowledge the spirituality and experiences that connect one actor with other actors. For this reason, we employed a PAR approach from a relational ontological perspective to work with Indigenous communities in relation to issues of relationality, dreams, hopes, expectations, and imagination. This research approach suggests that meanings of sustainability are connected to both the material and the spiritual world through everyday interactions with each other. It also takes a significant step in exploring identity and justice in relation to Indigenous understandings of sustainability (McKenzie et al., 2009).

Indigenous ways of knowing, doing, and learning have been ignored in many Indigenous regions and there has been minimal research on these intersecting issues locally or internationally (Tuck et al., 2014). Through the unique lens of relational PAR, this research tried to address this gap in an examination of postcolonial Indigenous communities' complex and shifting relationships to nature (Datta et al., 2015; Wilson, 2008) and in relation to discrimination and oppression regarding Indigenous environmental education and sustainability (UN Declaration, 2008).

Through imagining the future of both traditional education and our responsibilities as researchers, it became evident that collaboration and understanding participants' practices were key to the process of exploring the meanings of sustainability in an environmental education that values and enables the participants' community. Thus, the purpose and intention of this chapter is to acknowledge that an exploration of the meanings of sustainability from traditional relational and spiritual learning experiences is necessary. In beginning our research journey together it was critical to consider that we could not understand the community's sustainability perspectives solely through our relational PAR; however, we learned that our study could be understood as a step forward in decolonizing learning and reclaiming Indigenous ways of learning within Bangladesh state's education curriculum. This realization presented us with a rich context for developing collective research processes and informed an understanding that doing research that recognized Indigenous communities' collective rights (i.e., community and researcher both own research and research findings) meant respecting traditional and spiritual practices, honoring spirituality, sharing and learning stories, taking responsibility, and talking with participants about their education needs.

Community's environmental sustainability

In this chapter, the *community-based sustainability* that emerged from the data addresses participants' understandings of sustainability: their hopes, dreams, and responsibilities for sustainability in relation to environmental management. This chapter corresponds with the third research question: What are Laitu Khyeng hopes and expectations regarding land-, water-, and forest-management policies and practices, particularly in relation to environmental sustainability? Data analysis suggested two emergent themes that address this question: the community's understanding of sustainability (i.e., the community's views on sustainability and sustainability management) and the community's goals for sustainability.

Community's views on sustainability in relation to environmental management

Indigenous people have a broad knowledge of how to live and sustainably manage their environment (Berkes, 2003). In defining environmental sustainability, community participants explained that their understanding of sustainability involved collective actions, responsibilities, hopes, expectations, and inspirations, which are interconnected with their traditional land- and water-management practices, identity, and life. In addition, participants grounded their perceptions in a number of inter-related practices: traditional cultivation, spiritual practices, ancestor stories, voicing community needs, and dreams, hopes, sounds, and smells. During the data-gathering process, participants advanced recommendations to help alleviate problems, specifically advocating particular actions and interventions (both collective and individual).

When discussing the community's conception of environmental sustainability, the first important issue to address is their **traditional cultivation culture**. Elder Kosomo Prue Khyeng stated that the purpose of sustainability was "to protect our traditional cultivation culture." According to the Elder, the community's traditional cultivation culture serves several roles: to protect nature, to encourage everyday relational and spiritual practices, to preserve ancestors' stories, and to fulfill everyday needs. Coresearcher Mathui Ching Khyang, after talking to the community's Elders and Knowledge-holders, explained in her commonplace book why their traditional cultivation culture is an important foundation of environmental sustainability.

> Our traditional cultivation is our relationship with mountain, sun (i.e., it rises every day in our Mother Mountains' laps. It delights and inspires us – like an ongoing flame), land, culture, history, and traditions. Our traditional cultivation is not only for our people but also for our relationships.

A second key element of the community's understanding of sustainability is their **everyday spiritual practices**. Spiritual practices are described in the data as linked to the protection of natural resources and community members' lives. Elder Basa Khyeng explained, "The land and water are our god(s) who are able to protect us." Particular spiritual practices are devoted to each of the various spirits; these include the sun spirits, motherland spirits, forest spirits, water spirits, exchange spirits (traditional local market), and sacrifice spirits. Knowledge-holder Thui Khyeng shared a folk song explaining the interrelationship of spirituality and sustainability (translated by coresearcher participant Mathui Ching Khyang).

> Our Motherland God: please bless us, protect us, and give us food.
> Our Sun God: we love you; keep us in your blessing.
> Our Forest God: please give us strength to protect you.
> Our Animal God: please come back again.
> Our Plant God: please keep us in your lap.

Participants emphasized the role of **ancestor stories** as learning tools, shaping knowledge and practice related to sustainability. For Elder Basa Khyeng, ancestors' stories are about the community's traditional cultivation practices on various lands: plain land, forestland, jungle land, and water land. Similarly, coresearcher participant Mathui Ching Khyang explained that the ancestors' stories are about "how our ancestors had survived and protected their life on our motherland." Her contention, therefore, was that protecting the ancestors' stories is a significant part of cultivating sustainability within the community.

The most common point discussed by participants emphasized that sustainability is an everyday **relational practice**. Knowledge-holder Kasamong Prue Khyeng likened the community's relationship with their environment to a vital part of the body: "Like our heart, we have been dependent on our land and water." Participant observation revealed that every morning at an early hour members of the Khyeng community started their Jhum work with a prayer honoring their relationality (e.g., with the sun god, the water god, and the plant gods). The community believes that their daily relationship with the gods will help them to produce their food, protect their land, and fight evil. Elder Shoi Khyeng shared her thoughts on why it is crucial to protect relationships with the community's nature gods. She said, "Our relationality is to respect and honor our nature gods, such as our river, trees, stones, sun, Jhum, and moon. We feel our relationality in our heart. We believe our relationality can help us in any critical situation." Building on this, the Elder emphasized that if they were not able to practice their relationality, they would not be able to survive and protect their forests.

Advocacy for the community's needs is identified in the data as another significant requisite for sustainability. Female activist Hla Kray Prue Khyeng explained, "The community's needs are our sustainability," adding, "If we are able to speak-up for our needs, we will be able to achieve our sustainability." Hla Kray Prue Khyeng spoke to the community's Elders, Knowledge-holders, leaders, and youth participants during Jhum and plain-land cultivation and summarized in her commonplace book the community's needs for preserving sustainability.

> First, we need to continue our hard work to stop money-lending national and international agency businesses in our villages, such as: microcredit [social enterprise], NGOs, and private tobacco companies. For this we need research, local workshops for our Elders and Knowledge-holders regarding land-grabbing strategies and tobacco's negative effects. Secondly, I think, the Bangladeshi government can play a significant role in stopping tobacco companies as in other parts of Bangladesh. Thirdly, we need to get back lost land for our survival and spiritual practices so that Indigenous people have opportunities to cultivate and produce food. Last but not least, it is important to encourage our farmers to cultivate traditional plants on our land.

Dreams play an important role in understanding the community's land and water sustainability and cultural practices. Elder Okko Khyeng explained that dreams are interconnected with their everyday spiritual practices. The Elder further clarified her sentiment stating, "Our *Sopnos* [Dreams] are our mountain, sun, relationships, culture, history, and traditions. Our *Shopnos* [dreams] can be understood as our *shanirborota* [sustainability management]." Similarly, Elder Kosomo Prue Khyeng discussed that dreams and hopes are for both the human and nonhuman. Offering an example, he stated, "Our dreams are not only limited to human beings. Dreams are for everything, such as forest, animals, mountains, and so on." In addition to encompassing the human and nonhuman, Elder Shoi Khyeng explained, "Our dreams are for every visible and nonvisible member." She elaborated that visible members include humans, animals, birds, crops, land, insects, mountains, rocks, moon, sun, and water; the nonvisible members include feelings, winds, smells, sounds, spirituality, and so on. Elder Basa Khyeng added, "Everything has life and has the power to influence us and our interactions." Thus, according to Elders, dreams associated with sustainability are dedicated to protecting all visible and nonvisible family members.

The community's **hopes** are explained in the data as directly corresponding with the community's needs for sustainability management. For instance, Elder Basa Khyeng stated that their hopes concerning negotiation with the Bangladeshi government are to "get back our lost land, forests, and mountains." Knowledge-holder Ching Shao Khyeng expressed a desire to hold onto hope and not allow it to diminish: "We want our hopes to succeed. We do not want to lose our hopes like a sunset." The Knowledge-holder expressed his wish for the Bangladeshi government to observe the community's hopes and goals of sustainable management: "We are able to protect our land, water, animals, and forest by ourselves. We do not need outsiders [whose main intent is to make a profit]."

In the same way that the community's hopes and dreams are grounded in spirituality, participants explained that the community's sounds also carry spiritual meanings and are tied to sustainable management. Knowledge-holder Thui Jo Khyeng explained that the community's traditional sounds vary from mountain to mountain, village to village, season to season, day to night, and so on. Elder Okko Khyeng added that he feels a responsibility to protect their spiritual sounds and smells as part of realizing goals of sustainability. Coresearcher Nyojy U Khyeng illuminated that traditional sounds are interconnected with forest, plain land, and water, emphasizing the significance of sounds to the relational and spiritual connection with these elements.

> We grew up with waterfalls and mountain water sounds; these sounds mixed with our body and mind. We recognize our community's people and animals, even plants, by these sounds. We can find our community roots with waterfalls and mountain water sounds. Our sounds are relationships, our inspiration to live with our ancestors and our spirituality.

Coresearcher Hla Aung Prue Khyeng shared in his commonplace book that traditional sounds are impactful for sustainability management.

> The Bangladeshi government's land-management policy-makers do not see and/or cannot feel our traditional sounds. If we have opportunities to be educated in our culture and language, we will be able to teach our traditional management meanings of sounds to our future generations.

Elders and Knowledge-holders expressed that the community's traditional relationship with sounds plays a spiritual role in sustainability management. Elder Basa Khyeng outlined that the Khyeng community uses various kinds of sounds to go "hunting, planting, and dancing to protect from evil spirits." Similarly, Knowledge-holder Kasamong Prue Khyeng explained, "When the wind blows, it makes a spiritual sound. Our plants, animals, and our heart are dancing with the wind's sound. We have nothing but our relationships to avoid evil spirits."

Like sounds, the community Knowledge-holders explained during both individual and sharing-circle conversations that a spiritual connection to **smells** is also vital to land, water, and forest sustainability management. Participants explained that smell is regarded by the community as a source of inspiration. They further clarified that smells such as wild and domestic animals, crops, Jhum land, plants, and people have distinct meanings in their community. Because particular smells serve as a determining factor influencing the planting and harvesting of various kinds of crops in Jhum and plain-land cultivation, sustainable management practices rely greatly on traditional ties to smells.

In summary, according to participating Elders, Knowledge-holders, coresearchers, and leaders, understandings of sustainability within the community are grounded in traditional cultivation culture, spirituality, responsibility, relationality, and talking about community needs. The data also illuminated how the traditional significance of dreams, hopes, smells, and sounds are connected to sustainability and sustainability management. Participants explained that the above sustainability attributes are not viewed in a hierarchical manner but are mutually dependent. Participant views and understandings indicate a strong desire to protect the community's traditional cultivation culture, animals, Jhum, plants, land, and water.

Community's goals for building environmental sustainability

Participants expressed a number of goals for achieving sustainability for the community. Goals expressed by Elders, Knowledge-holders, and leaders included: the recognition of Indigenous identity by the state constitution; mainstream awareness of traditional land, water, and environmental management practices; an immediate halt to for-profit projects that exploit the community's cultivated and forestland; the reacquisition of lost forest, plain land, and cultivated land rights; the inclusion of Indigenous language in schools and educational institutions; the promotion of alternatives to tobacco; the inclusion of the community in land- and water-management decision-making processes; and inclusion in governmental and nongovernmental development projects and research. Elaborating on the goals listed above, community understandings regarding how to preserve and enhance the community's sustainability are discussed below.

The first goal discussed by participants is to enforce the protection of forest **species diversity**. Community Elders, Knowledge-holders, leaders, and youth participants stated that protecting forest species diversity is interconnected with the community's spirituality, culture, history, and tradition. Elder Okko Khyeng emphasized that the natural forest diversity is indivisible from culture, identity, stories, and traditions. Coresearcher participant Mathui Ching Khyang explained that it is the community's hope "to get back our traditional species that have been removed by different projects." She shared the following appeal, intended for the Bangladeshi government and development agencies: "Please help us to rebuild our natural forest. We need your help to stop discriminative projects from our land and get back our forestland. We (community people, forestland, plain land, animals, and plants) are like a family. Please give us our land back."

As emphasized by Knowledge-holder Thui Jo Khyeng, a second significant goal is to **eliminate poverty**. Elder Okko Khyeng explained, "It is essential we get back our rights to practice our traditional land and water management practices on our land to eliminate poverty from the community and to build a sustainable livelihood." According to the Elder, it is necessary for these rights to be codified within the constitution so that such rights may be invoked and enforced through established legal and judicial procedures. Elder Okko Khyeng connected the shift in state projects with the revitalization of traditional cultivation and the subsequent elimination of poverty within the community.

> Our customary land and water spiritual practices were weakened by the Bangladeshi government and nongovernment agencies. As a result of this, we have serious poverty in our community. Through our customary land and water spiritual practices, our traditional self-sufficient economy can be established.

Enforcement of the Chittagong Hill Tracts Peace Accord is a third main goal toward promoting the community's sustainability. The Chittagong Hill Tracts Peace Accord is a political agreement and peace treaty between the Bangladeshi Government and the Parbatya Chattagram Jana Sanhati Samiti (United People's Party of the Chittagong Hill Tracts), the political organization that controlled the Shanti Bahini (CHT Indigenous Political Party). The accord allowed for the recognition of the people and Indigenous of the CHT region and ended the decades-long insurgency between the Shanti Bahini and government forces (Adnan, 2004). Elders, Knowledge-holders, and leaders expect the Bangladeshi government, development agencies, researchers, educators, and mainstream people alike to take action to ensure the recognition of land rights established by the CHT Peace Accord. For example, Elder and leader Basa Khyeng explained why it is important that the peace accord succeed in enshrining land rights for the Laitu Khyeng community:

> We, as Indigenous peoples, have been protesting against the Bangladeshi government and non-government agencies' artificial land-management projects on our land for decades, but they didn't listen to us. Now, we need to protect our forest resources, plain land, and waters so that our children and grandchildren will have the ability to live. We need help from the global community to protect our life and our land. It is high time for all of us [Indigenous and non-Indigenous Bangladeshi] to come together and build a sustainable future. The support of land rights in the CHT Peace Accord can stand on our behalf. Today, we ask you to stand beside us and take action for the success of the Peace Accord.

Together, youth, Elders, leaders, and Knowledge-holders expressed that a fourth goal toward promoting sustainability is pressuring the Bangladeshi government to **immediately stop anticommunity development projects** in the community: Brickfield, tobacco plantations, and profit-oriented lumber plantations. Participants stated in the second sharing circle that the different agencies' development/management projects relating to the community's motherland are dangerous. Elder Kosomo Prue Khyeng expressed during the individual story-sharing process why the Bangladeshi government needs to stop for-profit projects on the community's cultivated and forestland immediately.

> Our food production and our children are at risk from different agencies' killing projects in our community. If the government does not stop these

dangerous *development* projects on our land, we will not able to protect ourselves, our future generations, and our environment.

It is clear from the data that the community's Elders, leaders, and Knowledge-holders believe it is essential to stop projects imposed by government and non-government agencies and begin to reverse the negative consequences experienced by the community.

The fifth goal articulated by participants is to **reclaim traditional forest and cultivated plain land**, which, according to Elder Kosomo Prue Khyeng, "have been forcefully taken from our community." Knowledge-holder Kasamong Prue Khyeng indicated that the three Laitu Khyeng Indigenous villages are the largest villages in Bandarban district and added that "80 percent of our forest and cultivated plain land have been grabbed by the Bangladeshi state government's Reserve Forest (RF) and the private agencies' for-profit projects." He went on to explain the need to get back lost lands.

> Every Khyeng family had 40–50 acres of land, which used to be sufficient for most of the family members' food consumption. Most of the time we had a surplus of food that we used to use during the next year. We were satisfied with our land, and we did not have a food crisis in our villages. However, since our lands and forest resources were stolen and/or grabbed by the government and the private companies' for-profit projects, we have been facing a serious food crisis in our community. Getting back our land from the state can solve our food crisis and poverty.

Similarly, Knowledge-holder Shangla Prue Khyeng explained how they aspire to rebuild their sustainability through the reclamation of stolen land. He said

> We want our land back. If we have our land back, we will be able to produce our own food and create our own sustainability. Our land is our sustainability. I would like to ask our government to please give our motherland back to us and save us and help us to protect our forest diversity.

The sixth goal illuminated by the data is an effort to persuade the Bangladeshi government to recognize the community's **customary practices as a key feature of their children's education**. Schoolteacher Ching Cho Khyeng explained that traditional cultivation culture needs to be institutionally recognized to ensure self-dependency and sustainability. He stated

> The state's institutional education systems teach incorrect information to our Khyeng Indigenous children and youth. This kind of education forces us to forget our culture so that we can be so-called *civilized*. I see this *civilized* as a dependency.

Community Elders and Knowledge-holders agreed that children should have the opportunity to learn traditional cultivation practices at a minimum until the fifth grade. Another Khyeng schoolteacher, Ching Shao Khyeng, explained sadly, "I wish we could have opportunities to tell our stories to other Indigenous and non-Indigenous communities. I think our education system can enrich us and can create opportunities to relate our stories to others."

The community's seventh key goal as emphasized by participants is to **determine and cultivate alternative crops to tobacco**. Knowledge-holder Kasa Mong Khyeng said, "We hope our government and development agencies will help us to promote tobacco alternatives for our community's villages." According to Elder Kosomo Prue Khyeng, the tobacco project has expanded within the last two decades. The Elder lamented, "Although we want to get out from this dangerous project's cultivation, most of us are stuck in the private companies' money-lending loop." Youth leader Hla Kray Prue Khayang reflected on the prospect of developing alternatives to tobacco plantations within the community. She explained that the Bangladeshi government and development agencies could play a significant role in promoting beneficial initiatives. Her expectations, articulated in her commonplace book, are as follows:

> First, we need to work to stop money-lending by private tobacco companies among our Indigenous peoples. For this, we need seminars and workshops to build consciousness. Secondly, the village farmers should ask individually for the land they need for cultivating food to survive. The Bangladeshi government and/or other development agencies, such as UNDP, UNESCO, and so on, should give financial incentives to our farmers for the first two years. These incentives, I propose, can be divided into three stages, such as: the first time when preparing the land, the second time when planting seeds, and the third time during plant growing. Thirdly, the money borrowed can be paid back within two or three years after harvest so that the farmer has kept the harvest for the family and surplus food can be used to pay back the loan. Finally, it is important to produce ginger and turmeric in our *Jhum* as these have economic value on the market and these products do not have negative impacts on *Jhum* and plain lands.

Hla Kray Prue Khayang proposed the above initiatives in order "to reduce poverty in her community."

The eighth goal outlined in the data promotes increased **involvement with government and development agencies' land and water management decision-making processes**. According to Elder Kosomo Priu Khyeng, the community endeavors to be part of management decision-making processes because, without community engagement, "the Bangladeshi government and non-government's land-management projects have become more exploitative than the British colonial government and the postcolonial Pakistani government." He also expressed the following grievance with various governing structures: "Neither the British colonial government [1757–1947] nor post-colonial governments [Pakistan 1948–1971 and Bangladesh 1972– current] have included us in our forest resource management or government reserve forest projects." Since Khyeng is one of the smallest Indigenous communities in CHT, Khyeng Elder Thui Jo Khyeng argued that they were more completely excluded from land-management decision-making processes than larger Indigenous communities. He stated sadly, "We got several management projects in our village; however, all of these projects were land-grabbing projects, they [different agencies] did not count our voice at all." This led Elders to state, "the Bangladesh government and others should first include our Elders and Knowledge-holders in our land and/or forest policy decision-making processes for our natural resource management."

It is evident from the data that the community has suffered land loss and poverty due to the Bangladeshi government, private companies, NGOs and development agencies' for-profit management projects. However, community members are not without hope. The community members have been fighting to stop different agencies' damaging projects and to protect Mother Nature. For example, Elder Basa Khyeng said, "We have observed that the community is not only dreaming and hoping but also working hard to rebuild its traditional forest-water management." Participants explained that the community not only has the ability to build a self-sufficient economy and protect local ecosystems, they are also able to contribute to the Bangladesh economy and create new forms of sustainable practice.

Through our conversations, the research team also learned that the Laitu Khyeng in CHT possess a robust sustainable management culture and can be a sustainable community. Even in tough times, they have worked to retain and regain the strength and gifts to help build their community. The community does not subscribe to the illusion that government will solve all of their challenges; rather, they recognize the importance of strengthening their own capacity as individuals and as a community. However, there are times when they need government, institutions, and multinational agencies to respond in meaningful ways to their sustainability needs.

The findings of this chapter suggest that although the current government's land-management projects are very different from the community's environmental resource management practices (see chapter 5), the community's meanings of sustainability are taken up in the form of knowledge and practice embedded in the Laitu Khyeng Indigenous community's local culture.

In addition, the findings show that participants in the study acknowledge that their community is facing many problems, but they are not treating the situation in a hopeless or pathologizing manner. Instead, they have been trying to protect their land, water, and forest. To achieve environmental sustainability in the community, participants recommended all the members of their community learn local traditional cultivation and practices for protecting the environment. In addition, it was suggested that the community should engage in both collective and individual actions.

Discussion

Although there is little agreement about what constitutes the term *sustainability*, the definition varying by scale, context, place, and time (Massey, 2005, 1994;

Vos, 2007), a number of studies have found that understanding community-based sustainability disrupts the binary opposition between Western (outsider) and Indigenous subjects – or the colonizers and the colonized (Amoamo & Thompson, 2010; Escobar, 2008; Whatmore, 2002, 2006). Since the Brundtland Report (1987) was issued, definitions of sustainability have tended to adhere to an economic paradigm in order to guide its meaning. The concept of sustainability has found its way into many vocabularies and into a variety of contexts. However, the dominant paradigm based on an economic model has become highly desirable and has a greater influence than parallel concepts, such as ecology, culture, and social sustainability (Geiser, 2001). Thrupp (1998) has argued that profit-oriented definitions of sustainability may be linked to ongoing threats to poor nations' sustainable livelihood. They also explained that in the dominant paradigm (i.e., economic profit) nature is seen as simply a resource of raw materials for the human economy. According to the authors, humans are viewed as being outside of nature and dominating it (see also Smith, 2006). All natural resources are available for human use, ideally as determined by market demand (Escobar, 1995; Hunington et al., 2006).

Study participants defined the term *sustainability* as the community's relational practices that served local members' interests and needs in a mutually beneficial way. Sustainability is a complex array of inter-related relationships with natural resources: relationships founded on a notion that all components are living beings and important for their mutual physical, mental, and spiritual survival and wellbeing. Such relationships are often reflected in and regulated by traditional rules and traditional legal systems, normally referred to as *customary Indigenous law*. The complex and diverse meanings of sustainability are imagined by participants as hybrid, situational, relational, and responsible.

The hybrid character of sustainable practice can provide insight into local environments in general (Altman, 2009). As Thrupp (1998) has argued, incorporating Indigenous hybrid practices into environmental sustainability can contribute to local empowerment and development, increasing self-sufficiency and strengthening self-determination. Escobar (2001, 2008) theorized how Indigenous hybrid and relational practices of land use are vital for Indigenous sustainable livelihoods. The Laitu Khyeng Indigenous community's everyday, practice-based sustainability aligns with Bhabha's (1991) vision of hybridity. As articulated by Bhabha, the community's management is situational and transformational with their everyday practices. We learned from participants' stories that the Laitu Khyeng Indigenous community's hybrid practices can offer the following diverse opportunities:

- Locally appropriate knowledge: Indigenous knowledge represents a way of life that has evolved with the local environment; thus, it is specifically adapted to the requirements of local conditions.
- Diversified production systems: There is no exploitation of a single resource. Risk is often mitigated by utilizing a number of subsistence strategies.
- Respect for nature: In Indigenous knowledge, the land is considered sacred, humans are dependent on nature for survival, and all species are

interconnected. Indigenous knowledge values all living beings (both human and nonhuman).
- Flexible: Indigenous knowledge is able to adapt to new conditions and incorporate outside knowledge.
- Social responsibility: There are strong family and community ties and with them feelings of obligation and responsibility to preserve the land for future generations.

Thus, the Laitu Khyeng's traditional hybrid management practices benefit from Indigenous knowledge as a foundation for effective sustainable practices (Altman, 2009).

A holistic perspective was discussed by participants as an important goal for explaining the community's sustainability. Participants relayed that a holistic approach combines Elders, Knowledge-holders, leaders, and youth: it brings together all the community's members to solve problems. Altman (2009, 2004) suggested that this holistic approach is about how people address local and regional development and the potential of multiple approaches in ensuring sustainability. In other words, participants discussed holistic goals as diverse "ways of imagining life" (Escobar, 2011, p. 139) by and for the local community.

According to participating Elders, Knowledge-holders, coresearchers, and leaders, the community's understanding of sustainability is grounded in traditional cultivation culture, spirituality, responsibility, relationality, and talking about community needs. The data also illuminates how the traditional significance of dreams, hopes, smells, and sounds are connected to sustainability and sustainability management. Participants explained that the above sustainability attributes are not viewed in a hierarchical manner but are mutually dependent. Participant views and understandings represent a strong desire to protect the community's traditional cultivation culture, animals, Jhum, plants, land, and water.

8 Youth responsibilities for sustainability

This chapter endeavors to illuminate why and how the community's youth wish to protect traditional land- and water-management practices to achieve environmental sustainability. Indigenous people of the community invited us all to understand the root causes of past and present problems and to take an active role in the healing process. They also defined what should be a caring youth based on the principles of collective ownership and sharing, mutual respect and helping within the extended family system and community, the acceptance of diversity, and collective responsibility for the well-being of all members of society, of future generations, and for the maintenance of all parts of Creation. The original law passed down from their ancestors crystallizes the sacred responsibility of Indigenous people to be the caretakers of all that is on Mother Earth; therefore, youth are responsible and are able to build new forms of environmental sustainability for all. The responsibilities of the community's youth are the driving force behind the development of Indigenous culture being reflected in the institutions and systems of Indigenous people: uplifting traditional cultivation culture, decision-making through consensus, division of labor respecting the respective roles of the clans and based upon need, survival and family structure contributing to sharing, social cohesion, and respect for life. Respect for people and for Mother Earth is linked together for people to survive and care for future generations.

The community believes that each animal and plant has something to teach us about our responsibility to the earth. For example, the tiny ant teaches us to focus, how to work collectively, to observe the world with all our energy and being, and to appreciate the wonder of our world. Deer teach us to walk quietly upon the earth and to live in harmony with its cycles. One has only to observe and to take the time to see with more than our eyes and our mind. These teachings were heeded very solemnly by the community's ancestors. The institutions and the relationships that developed over thousands of years of interdependence have become tied perennially to the people's psyche as Indigenous people. Elders and Knowledge-holders suggested that if there is to be a successful program of Indigenous sustainable development, it will be necessary for the community's youth to take responsibility for developing working relationships with community Elders and Knowledge-holders since it is they who have the most to contribute to innovative approaches for Indigenous peoples and sustainability. In building sustainability, both community Elders and Knowledge-holders think that the community's youth can take significant responsibility for bridging Western science and Indigenous knowledge by ensuring that the values of the traditional lifestyle are recognized and supported. According to community Elders and Knowledge-holders, youth responsibilities for sustainability will provide opportunities for the documentation, sharing, and integration of traditional knowledge within sustainability strategies.

An interesting development within the participatory research process was that as the youth became more comfortable with one another and with the process, they began asking follow-up questions to each other's responses. According to youth and coresearcher participants, youth understanding of sustainability is similar to that of Elders, Knowledge-holders, and leaders; however, they believe their views of sustainability carry a number of particular responsibilities. Actions and responsibilities identified in the data include: organizing peaceful movements; disseminating negative consequences to mainstream national and international (e.g., UN and other donor agencies) communities; critiquing state anticommunity educational curricula; learning traditional cultivation; promoting traditional music, dance, and songs; preserving and promoting Khyeng language; and protecting customary practices. Such actions and responsibilities are elaborated below through drawing on data from the participants' conversations.

Organize peaceful movements

To foster the community's sustainability, the youth's first responsibility is to organize peaceful movements aimed at preventing government and non-government land-management projects – Brickfields, for-profit plantations (lumber), and tobacco plantations – from being developed in the community. As part of the youth action mandate, female leader Mathui Ching Khyang asked, "Is there anyone in our government who can hear our cries for our motherland? Who can feel our pain for mother forest, mountains, water, and traditional cultivation?" The Khyeng student president, Hla Prue Khyeng, explained that if youth advocates are not able to stop the management projects, they may lose the opportunity to preserve their Indigenous identity, traditional cultivation culture, language, and spirituality. Through this action, youth wanted to reach out to government and other agencies in order to make heard their appeal on behalf of the motherland and the community's needs.

Learning traditional cultivation systems

A second responsibility discussed by youth participants is to learn traditional cultivation systems (see Figure 8.1). Coresearcher participant Nyojy U Khyang shared the following in his commonplace book: "We youth hope to learn cultivation processes from our Elders. We know our cultivation system can save our land, water, animals, birds, and our ecosystem. . . . We do not have enough

Figure 8.1 Traditional Jhum and plain-land cultivation. The top picture shows Jhum cultivation, and the bottom photo shows plain-land cultivation. The Laitu Khyeng Indigenous coresearcher participant Nyojy U Khyang explained that sustainability is learning traditional cultivation systems.

money, but we do have Elders and Knowledge-holders who can teach us how to protect ourselves and our environment." Youth participant Hla Aung Prue Khyeng stated in agreement, "Our traditional cultivation knowledge is our educational curriculum." Elder Shoi Khyeng reinforced the youth's desire to prioritize traditional knowledge stating, "We need to tell our traditional stories to our children so that our children are able to get educated and protect our Mother Nature."

Promotion of community music, dance, and stories

The third responsibility highlighted by youth in the data involves the promotion of community music, dance, and stories. Many of the youth participants expressed that the music, dance, and stories are important to building sustainability as they make up a significant component of the community's management knowledge system. Youth participant Usa Khyeng illuminated that music and dance were avenues of spiritual connection and that he needed to protect them for himself and the community. To illustrate his sentiment, the participant shared a folk song describing the community's relationships with plants, birds, animals, and so on. The song, which was written by Knowledge-holder Kasamong Prue Khyeng and translated by coresearcher participant Mathui Ching Khyang, is included below.

> My beautiful younger sister plants
> Do you hear? Your friends (birds) are singing for you.
> Do you hear? Your friends (deer) are singing for you.
> Do you hear? Our paddy crop is dancing with the wind for you.
> Do you see? I am making rice pitas for you.
> O my adorable sister.

Preservation and promotion of mother language

A fourth responsibility discussed in the data emphasizes the preservation and promotion of the Khyeng language. The youth participants explained that they have been actively lobbying to integrate their language into the education system. Youth participant Hla Aung Prue Khyeng expressed a hope that the Bangladeshi government will recognize the Khyeng language and "provide an opportunity to study until grade five in our language." Likewise, youth participant Nyojy U Khyang believes that revitalizing the Khyeng language will help community members to better understand their cultural cultivation system and more successfully protect their environment. Youth participant Usa Khyeng similarly expressed that preserving the community's language is connected to nurturing the community's sustainable lifestyle. The youth participant stated, "If we get own-language education, we are confident enough that we will be able to refuse all the unexpected management projects on our motherland." Highlighting the importance of the community's language, coresearcher participant Hla Aung Prue Khyeng indicated that proponents are already working with Khyeng Elders and Knowledge-holders to develop Khyeng writing scripts.

Protect traditional customary laws

The fifth responsibility addressed by youth participants emphasizes a need to protect traditional customary practices. Coresearcher participant Nyojy U Khyang explained in his commonplace book why the community's customary practices are important for their land and water sustainability management. He wrote, "Our traditional land and water management practices are our relationships; our practices are to us as sharing processes with each other and do not make our people as others." He went on to add, "We dance, sing, and solve the land problem according to our customary practices." Youth participant Usa Khyeng expressed a similar sentiment.

> Our customary land and water practices are different from the Bangladeshi government's and nongovernment's land-management projects; thus, the administration does not show interest in understanding our traditional land and water management system. Our customary land and water practices are vital for our identity and sustainability.

Learning traditional weaving

A sixth responsibility emerging from the data is a commitment to **learning traditional clothes-making techniques** associated with the community's traditional sustainability practices (see Figure 8.2). Coresearcher participant Hla Kray Prue Khyeng emphasized the connection between traditional clothes-making practice and cultural identity: "Our identity and culture are interconnected with our traditional clothes-making tradition." However, she added that governmental and nongovernmental land and water management projects contribute to the loss of the Khyeng community's traditional clothes-making education.

Similarly, highlighting the importance of traditional clothes-making knowledge for the community's sustainability, youth participant Usa Khyeng offered, "Our traditional clothes-making not only tells lots of our relational stories, but it also connects us with our ancestors' sustainability memories [i.e., self-sufficiency]."

Practicing spirituality

In developing sustainability, the youth want to honor, respect, and learn traditional spirituality, one of the most ancient and effective methods from their Elders and Knowledge-holders. Although dialogue among Elders and Knowledge-holders took many forms, specific types of structures were used and are still used today to promote spirituality practices according to individual and group initiatives. "Spiritual practice is premised upon the concept of respect, non-interference, and the recognition that the spirits of our grandfathers and the Creator are present to guide

Figure 8.2 Traditional clothes-making. This photo shows an indigenous Elder teaching their youth traditional clothes-making techniques.

us through the process," said coresearcher and youth Hla Kray Prue Khyeng. She also said that spirituality practices can provide places where Indigenous people can go to heal and renew mind, body, and spirit. These spiritual powers can provide places to which people can go to escape from racism, exploitation, violence, addictions, unemployment, and homelessness.

Protecting medicine people

In Indigenous Laitu Khyeng, there are specific Medicine People who are charged with the responsibility of understanding the healing qualities of the plants, animals, minerals, and spirits of the Indigenous environment. These people are afforded a special place around the fires because they have gone through a long and difficult process of training to be afforded the title of Medicine Person. It is not just a matter of learning the qualities of the plants and the minerals; the training consists of many years of preparing the spirit for this role through fasting and self-sacrifice. Protecting Medicine People and their knowledge can lead to protecting the history and legends of the people as a part of sustainability.

Networking

A ninth imperative recognized by the youth is to broadcast the negative consequences of the government and private agencies' land-management projects to the mainstream population by building a strong network of educators, scholars, policy-makers, practitioners, and activists. Coresearcher participant Hla Aung Prue Khyeng asserted, "We need to inform all Bengalis that, through the artificial management projects, our motherland, environmental diversity, and spirituality have been stolen from us as has our land," and further that, "We believe that if we are able to show correct information to the mainstream communities, our motherland and nature will be protected." Finally, the youth participant specified, "We need to build awareness [nationwide] through the media and news for stopping the Brickfield, the tobacco plantation, and the profit-oriented plantations in our community."

Developing educational curriculum

A tenth responsibility expressed by youth for promoting traditional sustainability is to correct the state's insufficient educational curriculum, which provides inaccurate information about Bangladeshi Indigenous communities' culture, natural resource management, cultivation, food, and identity. Coresearcher participant Nyojy U Khyang explained that the state educational curricula provided false and derogatory information about Indigenous communities, suggesting that, "we [Indigenous people] are uncivilized and our traditional culture, cultivation, and spiritual practices are anti-development, and so on." Aligned with Elders and Knowledge-holders, the youth community does not dispute that all children should participate in mainstream institutional education; however, they want the government's educational curricula to change and provide accurate information about their traditional management knowledge. Laitu Indigenous schoolteacher Mongla Prue Khyeng said that, although changing the state curriculum is a challenge, he is not deterred in his efforts. In addition to such advocacy, Mongla Prue Khyeng spoke of his involvement in an initiative to share traditional stories and knowledge to community children at home. Laitu Indigenous schoolteacher Nyojy U Khyang similarly emphasized efforts to amend state curricula: "The Khyeng and other Indigenous primary and high school teachers requested that the district change Indigenous communities' school curriculum." Participants highlighted in the data that they wanted cooperation from the Bangladeshi government in adding traditional knowledge to their current education curriculum. Nyojy U Khyang stated, "We want to learn our traditional knowledge first as we believe our traditional knowledge can help us to build relationships with our forest and spirituality." Participants aspired to keep alive their traditional stories, not only because they are a part of their traditional heritage, but also because the stories are essential to cultivating the community's sustainability.

In summation, the data revealed that the youth community was active and hopeful, driven by a dream of achieving sustainability goals through fulfilling a series of key responsibilities. The community youth believe that it is a critical moment for reclaiming their voice and rights and that, if they cannot, youth and future generations will soon lose their identity and sustainable livelihood.

Discussion

The Indigenous people and their youth were aware of their responsibility – not just in terms of balance for the immediate life – they were also aware of the need to maintain this balance for their environment. The youth's responsibilities in building sustainability suggest not simply adding on Western forms of management. The youth's dreams and hopes were of centering Indigenous ways of knowing with the new forms of sustainability where they can learn, act, and belong. Through these responsibilities, youth believe that they can overcome the severity of the state's environmental management crisis and lead to a radical departure from current development-dominated knowledge and education models.

From the situational and holistic views on sustainability, another main issue revealed in the study's findings involves youth's relational responsibilities. Youth see their relational responsibilities as protecting the community's traditional land-management practices and building a sustainable livelihood. According to the United Nations (2013), youth are one of the significant stakeholders for community development and sustainability. Similarly, Collins (2004) expressed that young people possess more significant power and potential today to create change on a global and local level than they have had in any previous generation. Likewise, others (e.g., Chawla 1998; Chataway, 1997; Tanner, 1980) have stressed that youth's collective responsibility as environmental leaders is important to their sustainability. In reflecting on their lives, Laitu Khyeng youth's sense of collective responsibility as leaders and role models is significant in achieving sustainability. Thus, meanings of sustainability as understood and practiced by the Laitu Khyeng Indigenous community are built around complexity, situatedness, relationships, and responsibility. These relational knowledge traits are an integral part of the physical, spiritual, and mental dimensions of the community's systems of values and norms.

We learned that the Laitu Khyneg community had become landless and poor in the last couple of decades as a result of the Bangladeshi government and private companies, NGOs, and development agencies' for-profit development projects. However, community members were not without hope; they have trust in their youth that their youth can offer new possibilities. Youth can fight for their traditional education rights and to protect Mother Nature. The meanings of sustainability to youth are continuing through their dreams, hopes, and hard work. Youth's hard works and dreams can offer new possibilities for Western environmental science to rebuild sustainability in the community, nationally, and beyond.

We also gained knowledge that their meanings of education not only had the ability to build a self-sufficient economy and protect their ecosystem but could also contribute to the state's management policies and create new forms of sustainability education practices. The youth responsibilities in Indigenous communities have the potential to inform Western environmental educators, researchers, policy-makers, and activists at a deeper and heightened level of understanding.

By combining these youth's responsibilities for Indigenous sustainability with the non-Indigenous environmental sustainability knowledge system, a strong new relationship, a strong new relationship will emerge between Indigenous and non-Indigenous peoples.

The development of Indigenous youth responsibility for their environmental sustainability evolved inside the family, community, and clan structure. This led to the development of a sense of responsibility that was actualized in a division of labor aimed at the benefit of the group. Each individual's activity with respect to survival was only one aspect of meeting the needs of the group. All members were expected to contribute for the benefit of the larger group. This interdependence was again a reflection of the lessons of nature gleaned from observations of the relationship of all living things to each other. In this relationship, there was not only equality with the other spirits of sustainability but also equality with all beings (both human and nonhuman) (Latour, 2004). No being (human or nonhuman) was any less than the other; each had a role to perform in creating sustainability. Each animal and plant was quite simply only a piece of the overall scheme of things and had something to contribute that was valued equally with all others. Indigenous Elders and Knowledge-holders explained the Indigenous youth's responsibility for their environmental sustainability as a **movement** which can provided opportunities for youth and their communities to explore the meaning of land-water management and its faculties – sources of wisdom, values bestowed, and voices harnessed in the process of place-making. Indigenous youth's responsibilities have a profound impact in facilitating the inclusion and recognition of Indigenous ways of protecting sustainability and its global impact.

The findings in this chapter confirm that Indigenous youth and their responsibility for environmental sustainability can have extensive positive value in protecting the land-water and traditional management and in building healthy, sustainable local economies with the wisdom and tools to strengthen their relationships to the land and to continue to decolonize their communities and environment.

9 A call to implications

Guiding principles for environmental sustainability

The observance of human rights, including land-water and natural resource–management rights, participation rights, and nondiscrimination rights, is critical to environmental sustainability. Secure Indigenous land-water rights not only bring environmental benefits, they can also foster economic development (Corntassel, 2012; McGregor, 2012; McCoy et al., 2016; Tuck & McKenzie, 2015). Pursuing Indigenous perspectives on land-water management today means struggling to reclaim and reconnect one's relational, land-based existence by challenging the ongoing, destructive forces of colonization. Whether through traditional land-water practices, ceremonies, or other ways that Indigenous peoples (re)connect to the traditional meanings of sustainability, processes of resurgence are often contentious and reflect the spiritual, cultural, economic, social, and political scope of the struggle.

If colonization is a disconnecting force, then reclaiming is about reconnecting with land-water, culture, and communities. Both decolonizing and reclaiming facilitate a renewal of our roles and responsibilities as Indigenous peoples to the sustainable praxis of sustainable Indigenous livelihoods, community governance, and relationships to the natural world and ceremonial life that enable the transmission of these cultural practices to future generations (Corntassel, 2012). North American Indigenous and non-Indigenous scholars Walker et al., (2013) book, *Reclaiming Indigenous Planning*, shows how reclaiming and reconnecting Indigenous people with their land-water facilitates reformulating planning practices to incorporate traditional knowledge, cultural identity, and stewardship over land and resources. They also suggest that since Western management planning outcomes in Indigenous communities have failed to reflect the rights and interests of Indigenous people, attempts to reclaim planning have become a priority for many Indigenous nations throughout the world.

To reclaim and reconnect with traditional Indigenous land-water rights and environmental resource management in the community, participants emphasized traditional ceremonies that, with little initiative, have relational outcomes such as youth Western and Indigenous bridging education, peaceful movements, learning traditional stories, and practice spiritualties. According to Elders and Knowledge-holders, everything has to be seen as relational action empowering youth in the community to learn the wisdom of both Indigenous and scientific knowledge in support of their shared goals. Such an emphasis is directed toward community members as well as educational and other governmental and nongovernmental stakeholders active within the region. Elder participants also recommended the restoration of Indigenous presence(s) on the land; the revitalization of land-water-based practices; and the transmission of Indigenous culture, spiritual teachings and knowledge of the land between Elders and youth.

Research and activism

This research was a form of activism for me. This researched changed who I am as a researcher and educator. It has empowered me through my research activities. In addition to our collective field research, I had opportunities to participate in a number of the community's activities and had numerous opportunities to join in different local and national Indigenous and minority land-water rights movements (e.g., land-water rights, stopping tobacco, Brickfield city demonstrations); disseminated research results to local audiences (e.g., governmental forest, land and CHT ministries, NGOs, Indigenous research organizations, university professionals, and practitioners), multinational agencies (UNDP, UNESCO, and Caritas), participated in international seminars and conferences (presentations in Canada, Japan, New Zealand, Norway, United States), and produced local and international journal publications (i.e., four commonplace books and three international journal articles).

Various peaceful demonstrations for Indigenous land and water rights aimed at stopping unwanted development projects have inspired me and deeply situated me in this research. From my previous relationships with an Indigenous student group,[1] I had the opportunity to know the CHT Indigenous leaders and activists. During our field research, I participated in three demonstrations: land and water rights, stopping the tobacco plantation, and Brickfield city demonstrations with CHT Indigenous leaders, student leaders, and activists in CHT, Bangladesh. During these demonstrations, I had the opportunity to meet and reconnect with different CHT Indigenous and minority community leaders, Elders, and activists. All three demonstrations were peaceful and involved a large participation. I have come to realize that undertaking this study is a political activity dedicated to the reclamation of Indigenous and individual (as an Indigenous and minority person) rights (Becker, 1967). Thus, I see that research is not neutral; rather it is grounded in both an academic and political responsibility to protect and reclaim our rights (which includes environmental resource management, sustainability, and identity).

Disseminating research results with various organizations was a significant and memorable political activity for a number of reasons. First, since our research was the first academic research study conducted with this community, many of the speakers were presenting on the topic for the first time. Second, we had the opportunity to present our research results and recommendations to Bangladesh forest, land, and CHT ministries. Bangladesh's CHT Ministry Secretary, Information Ministry Secretary, Dhaka University professors, and journalists were invited to be panel speakers. The attendees were from many backgrounds, such as NGOs, Indigenous research organizations, university professionals, multinational agencies (UNDP, UNESCO, and Caritas), and students. The full seminar was recorded and broadcast to a number of national TV stations and newspapers. We also presented at various international academic conferences. Community participants contributed to the presentations through Skype.

Another significant event that stands out upon reflection is re-establishing a previous professional relationship with the Association for Land Reform and Development (ALRD) to publish and organize a seminar free of charge.

Another activity that stood out for me in the research process was the production of four commonplace books by community members, which were subsequently provided to a range of stakeholders. Copies of these books were distributed to the Bangladesh Forest, Land, and CHT ministries, universities, NGOs, Indigenous research organizations, students, and multinational agencies.

Finally, through our continuous efforts to publish journal articles, we have published in three international journals and are working to publish in three more. To conclude this section, my reflections on conducting the study reveal instances where I acted as a learner and an activist, instead of as an observer, and became a more active participant.

In chapter 5, I discussed the main topics emerging from the data in response to this book research questions and addressed the topics in relation to the existing literature. I also offered suggestions for policy and practice and for future research in the context of Laitu Khyeng land and water practices and management. I have concluded the discussion of the research with a personal reflection on what the process has meant to me personally and professionally. The final section of this book considers how future research might be designed to further advance knowledge on the topic.

Implications for policy and practice

In this section, recommendations for policy and practice are presented together with brief explanations drawn from the data. The study results suggest that in order to realize environmental sustainability in the Laitu Khyeng Indigenous community, the following must be achieved:

- Protection of traditional cultivation culture and ways of life.
  - Government and nongovernment environmental resource management policies and practices that ensure protection for the traditional cultivation culture must be adopted.
  - Management policies and alliances must be formed with the Laitu Khyeng Indigenous peoples to defend their plain lands, forestlands, and water lands from exploitative development and to advocate for the resolution of outstanding issues, such as the CHT Peace Accord and land claims. There is a need to recognize the Indigenous administrative structure as

the resolution of these issues will strengthen the capacity of Laitu Khyeng peoples to protect their environmental resources and promote their sustainability.
- Indigenous people must be supported to defend themselves from unwanted development threats, including reserve forests, tobacco plantations, Brickfield industrial companies, and lumber plantations.
- Government and multinational environmental agencies must recognize the value of traditional knowledge and practices in Indigenous environmental resource protection and develop working relationships with Indigenous peoples based on their values and culture.

- The return of cultivated and uncultivated lands to the Laitu Khyeng community.
    - Lands grabbed from Indigenous peoples must be returned.
    - All lands illegally occupied should be recovered as soon as possible.
- Documentation and advancement of the Laitu Khyeng Indigenous community's traditional management culture and practices.
    - Traditional cultivation knowledge and practices must be documented and integrated into environmental resource management policies.
    - The traditional resource management administrative structure must be recognized as having equal authority and contribution to the state administrative structure.
    - A new standard of responsibility needs to be developed between researchers, institutions, and Indigenous peoples to guide access to traditional knowledge.
- Implementation of traditional knowledge-based environmental resource management education.
    - Indigenous people and traditional cultivation culture and practices must be included in the state education's institutional curriculum.
    - Traditional cultivation culture and practices must be recognized as equivalent to the state knowledge system.
- The design of development projects that adhere to Indigenous tradition and culture.
    - Development strategies must be based on Indigenous traditional culture and practice.
- Development of inclusive, participatory processes for generating development plans and policies.
    - Government and nongovernmental agencies must include Indigenous Elders, Knowledge-holders, leaders, and youth in their development plans and policies.

Implications for future research

As was pointed out in the introductory chapter, there is limited available research exploring Laitu Khyeng Indigenous natural resource management and sustainability, especially where the roles of traditional knowledge and practices are considered. Although the few studies conducted in the CHT region of Bangladesh concerning environmental resource management (e.g., Adnan, 2004; Roy, 2000) and sustainability (Chakma, 2010) address Indigenous knowledge, there is little to no research available on land and water management issues in the Laitu Khyeng Indigenous community. There is a strong need for further research in this area. Based on the research findings, the study highlights a need for further research, designed according to the considerations outlined below:

- As the literature review has shown, there are more than eleven Indigenous communities living in the CHT, Bangladesh. This research project addresses only one of these Indigenous communities. The first area for further research should be to investigate more Indigenous communities in order to expand and enrich understanding of the region. This must be undertaken through research questions and methodologies dedicated to protecting Indigenous traditional knowledge and culture and aligning with similar research conducted with other indigenous communities around environmental sustainability.
- This study suggests that traditional land and water resources are hybrid, relational spaces for vocational and spiritual practices connected with environmental sustainability. One possibility for further research would be to explore this by implementing the recommendations participants made about how environmental sustainability should be regained in the community. Because the Laitu Khyeng community is mostly dependent on their traditional cultivation culture, the recommendations would need to be integrated through state support.
- More research and support is needed around youth responsibility for achieving sustainability, including commitment demonstrated in state programming. For example, youth need support to learn traditional cloth-making, cultivation, and spirituality. Research programs could be designed around youth's sustainability goals that aid them in deciding which crops to grow and in identifying which environmental management practices and policies to use. Local Elders and Knowledge-holders can be utilized in delivering instruction.
- The contribution of traditional Indigenous knowledge in working towards environmental sustainability seems clear. This study has revealed that there is a clear difference between Indigenous ways of practicing sustainability and the government's ideas of development and sustainability. Because much of Indigenous knowledge and practice in Bangladesh is undocumented and could soon become extinct due to displacement and unwanted development projects, the study recommends further research documenting relevant CHT

Indigenous knowledge and practices related to environmental sustainability. It also recommends that such knowledge and practice be authentically represented in the institutional curriculum of formal education (e.g., primary school). Such knowledge and practice should be taught in a variety of ways and should utilize the community's Elders and Knowledge-holders.
- There is a need for more studies exploring the role of spirituality in sustainable land and water management. Elders in the study emphasized that youth should learn in school that, according to spiritual principles of management, humans and nonhumans are a collective and interdependent. Therefore, environmental management must respect both humans and nonhumans. More studies are required exploring how spirituality can provide a framework for illuminating and drawing insight from environmental sustainability practiced by communities in the CHT. Other studies could investigate the integration of spirituality into environmental resource management policies and practices and in formal and informal educational settings.
- This study explored participants' understanding of land, water and environmental management in relation to knowledge and practice. Future studies could focus on language, identity, and culture as they link with sustainability. For example, a future research project could examine how a community identifies with cultural tradition and how that identification affects their orientation to sustainability.
- Finally, our study has recommended compliance with the CHT Peace Accord; future studies could explore the sustainability link with the CHT Peace Accord. There could be comparison studies to find out how the CHT Peace Accord is significant for Indigenous identity, land rights, culture, and environmental sustainability.

Personal reflections

This research has touched me personally and professionally in many ways. It has enabled me to rebuild close relationships with the Laitu Khyeng Indigenous community through which I have come to learn of their rich culture, traditions, wisdom, celebrations, spirituality, and unique sustainable lifestyle. In this section, I present my reflections on the process of conducting the study under three headings: reflections on times when I took on the role of a learner, a researcher, and an activist.

Throughout this research, I have learned that research is a collective journey. Because our study was *with* and not *on* the participants, we collectively engaged with our research. Elder Basa Khyeng informed me that in the Laitu Khyeng Indigenous community's culture there is no such thing called *other*. The community used the term *we* to find similarities rather than a way to highlight differences between people. According to participants, the word *we* has insight, strength, and capability. Throughout this process, I have been anxious about doing research on what has been called *the other*. I was concerned about the exchange, or really the lack of exchange, that characterizes the whole history of writing about other people. The term *we* also became a process for this research: we talked, we discussed, we challenged, we encouraged, and we made suggestions. We have worked through our differences and tried to preserve those differences that highlighted important insights. Through this collective journey, I have built a relationship with this community, but I have also built a relationship with their struggle and made it our struggle.

My second significant learning outcome involved a spiritual and emotional connection with the Laitu Khyeng Indigenous people who opened their hearts and hearths to me. I am glad that as a researcher, and despite being a part of the Western academia, I can claim to go beyond the stigma in which most researchers are "armed with *goodwill* in their *front pockets* and *patents* in their *back pockets*" (Smith, 1999, p. 24). Elders who participated in our study inspired me during our research by saying, "Your voice is our voice; our struggle is your struggle. Collectively, we need to win." I have found a parallel spiritual understanding and practice with land and water in the community. The community members believe that land and water are their gods and parents and cannot be replaced with an alien patriarchal god (i.e., Islam). I am thus humbled and, at the same time, reformed and enriched by this community.

Throughout this research, I kept asking "Who am I and what am I doing here?" These feelings were an appropriate and necessary part of the collective research processes. The Elders taught me that I was not an outsider. I have been asked by Elders to "Tell our story to your people." This method helped me to find the answers regarding who I am and what I am doing. The following questions were important for positioning me in this journey and to realize that this journey begins in our hearts and heads: How do we change? What do we believe and feel? And, what do we need to learn?

Dreams for moving forward

If there is to be successful environmental sustainability, it will be necessary for key actors to develop working relationships with traditional peoples, youth, and their knowledge since it is they who have the most to contribute to innovative approaches for Indigenous peoples and environmental sustainability. According to community Elders and Knowledge-holders, a bridging program between Western and Indigenous traditional land-water is vital for making this dream successful. Within an Indigenous sustainability program, we need to ensure that the value of the traditional lifestyle is recognized and supported. It must provide opportunities for the documentation, sharing, and integration of traditional knowledge within environmental sustainability strategies.

Indigenous knowledge and traditional cultivation practices must be recognized since it is Indigenous people who will be responsible for the continuation of sustainable practices. The program must also recognize the critical place of Indigenous Elders and Knowledge-holders because they, as the child's first teachers, are central agents for the protection of sustainability culture. With this focus, the dream of environmental sustainability will meet its objectives through both direct and indirect means: directly through the establishment of working relationships with key actors in the Indigenous community and indirectly by strengthening their position to affect change at the local level through recognition of the value of traditional knowledge and the critical role of Indigenous these groups.

Note

1 I was Vice President of the Bangladeshi Indigenous and Minorities Student Rights Organization during 2003–2008.

10 Concluding remarks

This book's study was guided by a framework of relational ontology (Datta, 2015; Kovach, 2005; McCoy et al., 2014; Wilson, 2008, 2007) set within the context of the CHT in Bangladesh. In contrast with a singular Western research model, this methodology favors a model that is plural and reflects Laitu Khyeng culture, values, and sustainability traditions. To develop this theoretical framework in conjunction with the study data, we drew on the following four ideas: first, the concept of relationality articulated by Ingold (2011), Meyer (2001, 2008); Smith (2008), and Wilson (2008), including ideas introducing new ways of understanding actors and their interactions; second, the concept of hybridity through the works of Bhabha (2004), Little Bear (2000), and Whatmore (2006), including how this conceptualization may intersect with notions of a relational ontology; third, Said's (1993) concept of otherness; and, finally, Lévi-Strauss's (1998) concept of scientific knowledge. All four of these concepts challenge our fixed ways of knowing, doing, and acting by including traditional experiences and everyday practices as significant sources of knowledge. Such relational research framing opens up broader spaces for environmental resource management and sustainability. The study acknowledges that relationality is at its center. In this relationality, "Actors, both human and nonhuman, living and nonliving, and their actions are not only explained as relational but also as spiritually interconnected, which makes one actor responsible to the other actors" (Datta, 2015, p. 2). Thus, this relational theoretical framework is a plural space where both humans and nonhumans co-exist in a way that does not privilege one over the other (Cajete, 1994; Hultman & Taguchi, 2010; Latour, 2004).

This book has determined that the Laitu Khyeng community contains a potential blueprint for a new relational environmental management approach. Community participants are committed to learning both Indigenous and non-Indigenous cultivation knowledge and practices. However, Elders emphasized that both sets of knowledge should be given equal priority. The community's relational understanding of natural resource management is not only about traditional cultivation culture; it is also about understanding their nonhuman relationships, which include spiritual places, animals, water, food, clothing, and education.

To move toward environmental sustainability in the Laitu Khyeng community, Elders asserted that community youth need to learn more traditional cultivation

134 Concluding remarks

knowledge and practices and address water protection, food sovereignty, identity, and spirituality. Educational curricula should focus on traditional cultivation and cultural issues so that youth have the opportunity to learn about their own culture and cultivation. In addition to learning traditional cultivation culture, Elders and Knowledge-holders also emphasized that youth education should be linked with spiritual and relational knowledge, which is the base of their traditional sustainability.

The book has examined the continuing destructive impacts of colonialism in the CHT, including specifically within the Laitu Khyeng Indigenous community, through analysis of the following processes: privileging governmental and nongovernmental management policies over traditional Indigenous management practices and privileging outsiders' Brickfield industrial projects, tobacco plantations, and lumber plantations. These revelations speak to the importance of engaging counter-hegemonic approaches as frames of analysis. Considering that colonialism is still prevalent in the region, it is crucial that issues of colonial management and development policies be resolutely confronted from a critical orientation that challenges the status quo. This study thus applied a relational theoretical framework with an emphasis on processes of challenging, decolonizing, and reclaiming traditional cultivation knowledge and practices.

Another important implication of the study involves the potential for building sustainability by recommending changes to current land-, water-, and natural-resource-management policies and practices. Even though CHT Indigenous traditional hybrid management practices have been locally relevant, scientific, and sustainable – empowered through local environmental management decision-making – the practices have been ignored in current governmental and nongovernmental natural resource management policies and actions. This research investigated how Indigenous land, water, and management knowledge, policies, and practices are needed in the Laitu Khyeng Indigenous community to promote environmental sustainability. The research makes a significant contribution to the existing literature in general as well as contributing to the future of environment-related educational practices in Bangladesh and similar contexts.

References

Adams, K., Burns, C., Liebzeit, A., Ryschka, J., Thorpe, S., & Browne, J. (2012). Use of participatory research and photo-voice to support urban Aboriginal healthy eating. *Health and Social Care in the Community, 20*(5), 497–505. doi: 10.1111/j.1365-2524.2011.01056.

Adnan, S. (2004). *Migration land alienation and ethnic conflict: Causes of poverty in the Chittagong Hill tracts of Bangladesh*. Dhaka, Bangladesh: Research & Advisory Services.

Adnan, S., & Dastidar, R. (2011). *Mechamisms of land alienation of the Indigenous peoples of the Chittagong Hill tracts, report of study undertaken for the Chittagong Hill tracts commission*. Copenhagen: International Workgroup for Indigenous Affairs (IWGIA).

Ahmed, B. (2012). Margin, minorities and a political economy of displacement: The Chittagong Hill tracts of Bangladesh. In R. Ganguly-Scarse & K. Lahiri-Dutt (Eds.), *Rethinking displacement: Asia Pacific perspectives* (pp. 173–194). Farnham: Ashgate.

Agrawal, A. (2002). Indigenous knowledge and the politics of classification. *International Social Science Journal, 54*, 287–297.

Agyeman, J., Bullard, D. R., & Evans, B. (2003). Conclusion: Towards just sustainabilities: Perspectives and possibilities. In J. Agyeman, R. D. Bullard, & B. Evans (Eds.), *Just sustainability: Development in an unequal world* (pp. 323–335). London: Earthscan Publications Ltd.

Aikenhead, G., & Michell, H. (2011). *Bridging cultures: Indigenous and scientific ways of knowing nature*. Toronto, ON: Pearson Canada.

Aikenhead, G. S., & Ogawa, M. (2007). Indigenous knowledge and science revisited. *Cultural Studies of Science Education 2*, 539–620. http://dx.doi.org/10.1007/s11422-007-9067-8

Altman, J. (2004). Indigenous affairs at a crossroads. *Australian Journal of Anthropology, 15*(3), 306–308.

Altman, J. (2009). The hybrid economy as political project: Reflections from the Indigenous estate', Keynote address to the *indigenous participation in Australian economies conference*, 9 November 2009, Canberra. Retrieved from <www.nma.gov.au/audio/detail/the-hybrid-economy-as-political-project>.

Amoamo, M., & Thompson, A. (2010). (Re) imaging Maori tourism: Representation and cultural hybridity in postcolonial New Zealand. *Tourist Studies, 10*(1), 35–55.

Amoamo, M., & Thompson, A. (2012). (Re) imaging Maori tourism: Representation and cultural hybridity in postcolonial New Zealand. *Tourist Studies, 10*(1), 35–55.

Ashcroft, B., Griffiths, G., & Tiffin, H. (1998). *The empire writes back: Theory and practice in post-colonial literatures*, London: Routledge.

References

Baker. T. A., & Wang C. C. (2006). Photovoice: Use of a participatory action research method to explore the chronic pain experience in older adults. *Qualitative Health Research, 16*, 1405–1415. doi: 10.1177/1049732306294118.

Banerjee, A. K. (2000). Devolving forest management in Asia-Pacific countries. In T. Enters, P. B. Durst, & M. Victor (Eds.), *Decentralization and devolution of forest management in Asia and the Pacific*. RECOFTC Report 18, RAP Publication 2000/1, Bangkok.

Barnhardt, R., & Kawagley, A. O. (2003). Indigenous knowledge systems and Alaska native ways of knowing. *Anthropology and Education Quarterly, 36*, 8–23.

Battiste, M. (2000). Maintaining aboriginal identity, language, and culture in modern society. In M. Battiste (Ed.), *Reclaiming Indigenous voice and vision* (pp. 192–208). Toronto, Ontario: UBC Press.

Battiste, M. (2008). Research ethics for protecting Indigenous knowledge and heritage: Institutional and researcher responsibilities. In N. K. Denzin, Y. S. Lincoln, & L. T. Smith (Eds.), *Handbook of critical and Indigenous methodologies* (pp. 497–509). Berkeley, CA: Sage.

Battiste, M., (2013). *Decolonizing education: Nourishing the learning spirit*. Saskatoon, SK: Purich Press.

Battiste, M., & Henderson, J. Y. (2000). *Protecting Indigenous knowledge and heritage: A global challenge* (pp. 23–34). Saskatoon: Purich.

Baum, F., MacDougall, C., & Smith, D. (2006). Participatory action research. *Journal of Epidemiology and Community Health, 60*, 854–857. doi: 10.1136/jech.2004.028662.

Becker, H. (1967). Whose side are we on? *Social Problems, 14*(3), 234–247.

Berkes, F. (1999). *Sacred ecology: Traditional ecological knowledge and resource management*. Philadelphia, PA: Taylor and Francis.

Berkes, F. (2003). Alternatives to conventional management: Lessons from small-scale fisheries. *Environments, 31*, 5–19.

Berkes, F. (2008). Evolution of co-management: Role of knowledge generation, bridging organizations and social learning. *Journal of Environmental Management, 90*, 1692–1702. http://dx.doi.org/10.1016/j.jenvman.2008.12.001

Berkes, F. (2009). Indigenous ways of knowing and the study of environmental change. *Journal of the Royal Society of New Zealand, 39*, 151–156.

Berkes, F., & Folke, C. (1998). *Linking social and ecological systems: Management practices and social mechanisms for building resilience*. Cambridge, UK: Cambridge University Press.

Berkes, F., & T. Henley (1997). Co-management and traditional knowledge: Threat or opportunity? *Policy Options, 18*(2), 29–31.

Bhabha, H. (1991). The Third Space: Interview with Homi K Bhabha. In J. Rutherford (Ed.), *Identity: Community, culture, difference* (pp. 207–21). London: Lawrence & Wishart.

Bhabha, H. (1996). Culture's in-between. In S. Hall & P. du Gay (Eds.), *Questions of cultural identity*, (53–60). London: Sage. Bhabha, H. K. (1985). Signs taken for wonders: Questions of ambivalence and authority under a tree outside of Delhi. *Critical Inquiry, XII*(1), 89–106.

Bhabha, H. K. (2004). *The location of culture*. London and New York, NY: Routledge.

Bloch, M. (2008). People into places: Zafimaniry concepts of clarify. In M. Dove & C. Carpenter (Eds.), *Environmental anthropology: A historical reader* (pp. 425–435). Oxford: Blackwell Publishing.

Boeije, H. (2010). *Analysis in qualitative research*. London: Sage.

Bohensky, E. L., & Maru, Y. (2011). Indigenous knowledge, science, and resilience: What have we learned from a decade of international literature on "integration"? *Ecology and Society 16*(4), 6. http://dx.doi.org/10.5751/es-04342-160406.

Borrini-Feyerabend, G., Kothari A., & Oviedo, G. (2004). *Indigenous and local communities and protected areas*. Cardiff and Cambridge, UK: Cardiff University and IUCN.

Bowers, C. A. (2006). *Revitalizing the commons: Cultural and educational sites of resistance and affirmation*. Langham, MA: Lexington Books.

Brightman, R. A. (1993). *Grateful prey: Rock Cree human animal relationships*. Berkeley, CA: University of California Press.

Brundtland Report. (1987). *Towards sustainable development in our common future*. Oxford: Oxford University Press.

Bunnell, F. (2008). Indicators for sustaining biological diversity in Canada's most controversial forest type: Coastal temperate rainforest. *Ecological Indicators, 8*, 149–157.

Butt, G., & McMillan, D. (2009). Clayoquot sound: Lessons in ecosystem-based management implementation from an industry perspective. *BC Journal of Ecosystems and Management, 10*(2), 13–21. Retrieved from www.forrex.org/publications/jem/ISS51/vol10_no2_art2.pdf.

Cahill, C. (2007). Afterword: Well positioned? Locating participation in theory and practice. *Environment and Planning, 39*(12), 2861–2865.

Cajete, G. (1994). *Look to the mountain: An ecology of indigenous education*. Durango, CO: Kivaki Press.

Cajete, G. (2000) Indigenous knowledge: The Pueblo metaphor of Indigenous education. In M. Battiste (Ed.) *Reclaiming Indigenous voice and vision*, (pp. 192–208). Vancouver: University of British Columbia Press.

Castellano, M. B. (2002). Updating aboriginal traditions of knowledge. In: G. J. Sefa, B. L. Hall, & D. G. Rosenberg (Eds.). *Indigenous knowledge in global contexts: Multiple readings of our world* (pp. 21–36). Toronto: University of Toronto.

Chakma, B. (2010). The post-colonial state and minorities: Ethnocide in the Chittagong Hill tracts, Bangladesh. *Commonwealth & Comparative Politics, 48*(3), 281–300.

Chang, H. (2008). *Autoethnography as method*. Walnut Creek, CA: Left Coast.

Chapola, J. (2008). *Labour migration, inter-ethnic relations and empowerment, a study of khyang indigenous garments workers, Chittagong Hill tracts, Bangladesh*. Bergen, Norway: University of Bergen.

Chataway, C. J. (1997). An examination of the constraints on mutual inquiry in a participatory action research project. *Journal of Social Issues, 53*, 747–765.

Chawla, L. (1998). Significant life experiences revisited: A review of research on sources of environmental sensitivity. *The Journal of Environmental Education, 29*(3), 11–21.

Chowdhury, K. (2008). Politics of identities and resources in Chittagong Hill tracts, Bangladesh: Ethnonationalism and/or indigenous identity. *Asian Journal of Social Science, 36*, 57–78. doi: 10.1163/156853108X267567.

Christopher, S., Watts, V., McCormick, A. V., & Young, S. (2008). Building and maintaining trust in a community-based participatory research partnership. *American Journal of Public Health, 98*(8), 1398–1406.

Clarkson, L., Morrisette, V., & Regallet, G. (1992). *Our responsibility to the seventh generation: Indigenous peoples and sustainable development*. Winnipeg: International Institute for Sustainable Development.

Cohen, L., Manion, L., & Morrison, K. (Eds.) (2000). *Research methods in education*. London: Routledge.

References

Collins, S. (2004). Ecology and ethics in participatory collaborative action research: An argument for the authentic participation of students in educational research. *Educational Action Research, 12*(3), 347–362.

Coombes, B., Johnson, J., & Howitt, R. (2012). Indigenous geographies I: Mere resource conflicts? The complexities in Indigenous land and environmental claims. *Progress in Human Geography, 36*(6), 810–821.

Corntassel, J. (2012). Re-envisioning resurgence: Indigenous pathways to decolonization and sustainable self-determination. *Decolonization: Indigeneity, Education & Society, 1*(1), 86–101.

Creswell, J. W. (2007). *Qualitative inquiry and research design: Choosing among five traditions*. Thousand Oaks, CA: Sage.

Darbyshire, P., MacDougall, C., & Schiller, W. (2005). Multiple methods in qualitative research with children: More insight or just more? *Qualitative Research, 5*, 417–436.

Datta, R. (2015). A relational theoretical framework and meanings of land, nature, and sustainability for research with indigenous communities. *Local Environment: The International Journal of Justice and Sustainability, 20*(1), 102–113. doi: 10.1080/13549839.2013.818957.

Datta, R., Khyang, U. N., Khyang, H. K. P., Kheyang, H. A. P., Khyang, M. C., & Chapola, J. (2014). Understanding indigenous sustainability: A community-based participatory experience. *Revista Brasileira de Pesquisa em Educação em Ciências, 14*(2), 99–108.

Datta, R., Khyang, U. N., Khyang, H. K. P., Kheyang, H. A. P., Khyang, M. C., & Chapola, J. (2015). Participatory action research and researcher's responsibilities: An experience with indigenous community. *International Journal of Social Research Methodology, 18* doi: 10.1080/13645579.2014.927492.

Davison, A. (2008). Contesting sustainability in theory – practice: In praise of ambivalence. *Continuum: Journal of Media & Amp; Cultural Studies, 22*(2), 191–199. doi: 10.1080/10304310701861598.

Debnath, K. M. (2010). *Living on the edge: The predicament of a rural indigenous santal community in Bangladesh*. (Doctor of Education Thesis). Toronto, Ontario: University of Toronto Press.

Dei, G. J. S. (1999). Local knowledge and educational reforms in Ghana. *Canadian and International Education, 29*(1), 37–71.

Dei, G. J. S. (2011). Introduction. In G. J. S. Dei (Ed.), *Indigenous philosophies and critical education: A reader* (pp. 1–15). New York, NY: Peter Lang.

Dei, G. J. S. (2002). Spiritual knowing and transformative learning. In E. V. O'Sullivan, A. Morrell, & M. O'Connor (Eds.), *Expanding the boundaries of transformative learning: Essays on theory and praxis* (pp. 121–132). New York: Palgrave.

Dei, G. J. S. (2013). Critical perspectives on Indigenous research. *Socialist Studies, 9*(1).

Deleuze, G. (2004). *The logic of sense*. London: Continuum.

Deleuze, G., & Guattari, F. (2004). L'Anti-Oedipe. Paris: Minuit. Translated as *Anti-Oedipus* by Robert Hurley, Mark Seem, and Helen R. Lane. London: Athlone, 1984.

Deloria, A. (1995). *Red earth, white lies: Native Americans and the myth of the scientific fact*. New York: Scribner.

Denzin, N. K., & Lincoln, Y. S. (2008). Introduction: The discipline and practice of qualitative research. In N. K. Denzin & Y. S. Lincoln (Eds.), *Strategies of qualitative inquiry* (pp. 1–44). Thousand Oaks, CA: Sage.

Deyhle, D. (2009). *Reflections in place: Connected lives of Navajo women*. Tucson: University of Arizona Press.

Dove, M. (2006). Indigenous people and environmental Politics. *Annual Review of Anthropology 35*, 191–208.

References

Dudgeon, R. C., & Berkes, F. (2003). Local understandings of the land: Traditional ecological knowledge and indigenous knowledge. In H. Selin (Ed.), *Nature across cultures* (pp. 75–96). Dordrecht: Kluwer.

Escobar, A. (1995). Power and visibility: Tales of peasants, women, and the environment. In A. Escobar (Ed.), *Encountering development: The making and unmaking of the third world* (pp. 154–211). Princeton, NJ: Princeton University Press.

Escobar, A. (1996). Constructing management: Elements for a poststructuralist political ecology. In P. Richard & W. Michael (Ed.), *Liberation ecologies: Environment, development, social movements* (pp. 46–68). London: Routledge.

Escobar, A. (1999). After management: Steps to an antiessentialist political ecology. *Current Anthropology, 40*(1), 1–30.

Escobar, A. (2008). *Territories of difference: Place, movements, life, redes*. London: Duke University Press.

Escobar, A. (2010). Latin America at a crossroads. *Cultural Studies, 24*(1), 1–65. doi: 10.1080/0950238090342420.

Escobar, A. (2011). Sustainability: Design for the pluriverse. *Development, 54*(2), 137–140.

Fairhead, J., & Leach, M. (1997). Cultural trees: Socialized knowledge in the political ecology of Kissia and Kuranko Island of Guinea. In K. Seeland (Ed.), *Management is culture: Indigenous knowledge and socio-cultural aspects of trees and forests in non-European culture* (pp. 7–19). London: Intermediate Technology Publication.

Ferreira, M. P., & Gendron, F. (2011). Community-based participatory research with traditional and indigenous communities of the Americas: Historical context and future directions. *International Journal of Critical Pedagogy, 3*(3), 153–168.

Fletcher, R. (2008). Ecotourism discourse: Challenging the stakeholders theory. *Journal of Ecotourism, 8*(3), 269–285.

Folke, C., Berkes, F., & Colding, J. (1998). Ecological practices and social mechanisms for building resilience and sustainability. In F. Berker & C. Folke (Eds.), *Linking social and ecological systems: Management policies and social mechanism for building resilience* (pp. 414–436). London: The University of Cambridge.

Forsyth, T. (1996). Science, myth and knowledge: Testing himalayan environmental degradation in Thailand. *Geoforum, 27*, 375–392.

Foucault, M. (1979). *The history of sexuality,* London: Allen Lane.

Freire, P. (2000). *Pedagogy of the oppressed*. New York, NY: Bloomsbury.

Gandhi, L., (1998). *Postcolonial theory: A critical introduction*. New Delhi: Oxford University Press.

Geiser, K. (2001). *Materials matter: Toward a sustainable materials policy*. Cambridge, MA: The MIT Press.

Getty, G. A. (2010). The journey between Western and Indigenous research paradigms. *Journal of Transcultural Nursing, 21*(1), 5–14.

Glass, K. C., & Kaufert, J. (2006). Research ethics review and aboriginal community values: Can the two be reconciled? *Journal of Empirical Research on Human Research Ethics, 2*(2), 25–40.

Gomes, A. (2004). *Looking for money: Capitalism and modernity in an Orang Asli village*. Melbourne: Center for Orang Asli Concerns Trans Pacific Press.

Gray, J. S. (2000). The measurement of marine species diversity, with an application to the benthic fauna of the Norwegian continental shelf. *Journal of Experimental Marine Biology and Ecology, 250*, 23–49.

Greenwood, M. L. (2009). *Places for the good care of children: A discussion of Indigenouscultural consideration and early childhood in Canada and New Zealand*. (Unpublished Doctoral Dissertation). Vancouver: University of British Columbia.

Haluza-Delay, R., O'Riley, P., Agyeman, J., & Cole, P. (Eds.) (2009), *Speaking for ourselves: Environmental justice in Canada*. Vancouver: UBC Press.

Haraway, D. (2004). The promises of monsters: A regenerative polities for inappropriate/d others. In D. Haraway (Ed.) *The Haraway reader*. New York: Routledge, 48–67.

Houde, N. (2007). The six faces of traditional ecological knowledge: Challenges and opportunities for Canadian co-management arrangements. *Ecology and Society, 12*(2), 34. http://www.ecologyandsociety.org/vol12/iss2/art34/

Human Right Congress for Bangladesh Minorities Report. (2011, June). Bangladesh's Hindus are dying. Are we okay with letting it happen? Dallas, Texas.

Human Right Congress for Bangladesh Minorities Report. (2013, June). Bangladesh's Hindus are dying. Are we okay with letting it happen? Dallas, Texas.

Human Right Watch. (2014). *Bangladesh: Country summary*. NY: Human Right Watch.

Hunington, H. P., Trainor, S., Natcher, D. C., Hungtington, O., & Chapin, T. S. (2006). The significance of context in community-based research: Discussion about fire. *Ecology and Society, 11*(1), 40.

Ingold, T. (2011). *Being alive: Essays on movement, knowledge and description*. London: Routledge.

Internal Displacement Monitoring Centre Report. (2015, June 16). *Bangladesh: Indigenous people and religious minorities still affected by displacement*. Oslo: Norway: Norway Refuge Council.

Internal Displacement Monitoring Centre Report. (2018, June 16). *Bangladesh: Indigenous people and religious minorities still affected by displacement*. Oslo: Norway Refuge Council. Retrieved from http://www.internal-displacement.org/publications/2006/bangladesh-minorities-increasingly-at-risk-of-displacement.

Iva, A. I. (2010). *Status of minorities in Bangladesh*. Dhaka, Bangladesh: Annual Report from SAHR.

Jashimuddin, M., & Inoue, M. (2012). Management of village common forests in the Chittagong Hill tracts of Bangladesh: Historical background and current issues in terms of sustainability. *Open Journal of Forestry, 2*, 121–137. doi: 10.4236/ojf.2012.23016.

Johnson, J. T., & Murton, B. (2007). Re/Placing native science: Indigenous voices in contemporary constructions of management. *Geographical Research, 45*, 121–129. doi: 10.111/j.1745-5871.2007.00442.x.

Kabeer, N. (2000). *The power to choose: Bangladeshi women and labour market decisions in London & Dhaka*. New York, NY: Verso.

Kabeer, N. (2011). Between affiliation and autonomy: Navigating pathways of women's empowerment and gender justice in rural Bangladesh. *Development and Change, 42*(2), 499–528.

Kapoor, K. (2008). *The postcolonial politics of development*. New York, NY: Routledge.

Kesby, M. (2005). Re-theorising empowerment-through-participation as a performance in space: Beyond tyranny to transformation. *Signs: Journal of Women in Culture and Society, 30*(4), 2037–2065.

Koukkanen, R. (2000). Towards an indigenous paradigm from a Sami perspective. *Canadian Journal of Native Studies, 20*(2), 411–436.

Kovach, M. (2005). Emerging from the margins: Indigenous methodologies. In L. Brown & S. Strega (Eds.), *Research as resistance: Critical, indigenous, and anti-oppressive approaches* (pp. 19–36). Toronto, Ontario: Canadian Scholars Press.

Kovach, M. (2009). *Indigenous methodologies: Characteristics, conversations, and contexts*. Toronto, Ontario: University of Toronto Press.

Kovach, M. (2010). Conversational method in indigenous research. *First People Child and Family Review*, 5(1), 40–48.

Kraidy, M. M. (2002). Hybridity in culture globalization. *Communication Theory*, 12, 316–339.

Latour, B. (1991). Technology is society made durable. In J. Law (Ed.), *Sociology of monsters: Essays on power, technology and domination* (pp. 103–131). London: Routledge.

Latour, B. (1999). *On recalling ANT' in actor network theory*. Oxford: Blackwell Publishing.

Latour, B. (2000). When things strike back: A possible contribution of 'science studies' of the social science. *British Journal of Sociology*, 51(1), 107–123.

Latour, B. (2004). *Polities of management: How to bring the sciences into democracy* (Catherine Porter Trans.). London: Harvard University Press (original work published 2004).

Lauer, M., & Aswani, S. (2009). Indigenous ecological knowledge as situated practices: Understanding fishers' knowledge in the western Solomon Islands. *American Anthropologist*, 111, 317–329.

Law, J. (2004). *Enacting management cultures: A note from STS*. Lancaster University: Centre for Science Studies. Retrieved from www.lancs.ac.uk/fass/sociology/papers/law-enactingmanagementcultures.

Lertzman, D., & Vredenburg, H. (2005). Indigenous peoples, resource extraction and sustainable development: An ethical approach. *Journal of Business Ethics*, 56, 239–254.

Lertzman, D. A. (2010). Best of two worlds: Traditional ecological knowledge and western science in ecosystem-based management. *BC Journal of Ecosystems and Management*, 10(3), 104–126. Retrieved from www.forrex.org/publications/jem/ISS52/ vol10_no3_art10.pdf.

Lévi-Strauss, C. (1998). *The savage mind: The management of human society*. Chicago: The University of Chicago Press.

Lincoln, Y. S., & Guba, E. G. (1985). *Naturalistic inquiry*. Newbury Park, CA: Sage Publications.

Little Bear, L. (2000). Jagged worldviews colliding. In M. Battiste (Ed.), *Reclaiming Indigenous voice and vision* (pp. 77–85). Vancouver, BC: UBC Press.

Loffler, L. G. (1991). *Ecology and human rights: Two papers on the CHT, Bangladesh*. 1991, Zurich, (mimeo).

Lovell, H. (2007). *More effective, efficient and faster? The role of non-state actors at UN climate negotiations*. (Tyndall Briefing Note 24, December 2007).

Martusewicz, R. (2009). Educating for 'collaborative intelligence': Revitalizing the cultural and ecological commons in Detroit. In M. Mckenzie, P. Hart, H. Bai, & B. Jickling (Eds.), *Fields of green – Restorying, culture, environment and education* (pp. 253–267). Cresskill, NJ: Hampton.

Massey, D. (1994). *Space, place and gender*. Cambridge, MA: University of Minnesota.

Massey, D. (2005). *For space*. London and Thousand Oaks, CA: Sage.

McCarthey, S., & Moje, B. E. (2002). Identity matters. *Reading Research Quarterly*, 37(2), 228–238.

McCoy, D. T., Tan, I., Hartmann, D. L., Zelinka, M. D., & Storelvmo, T. (2016). On the relationships among cloud cover, mixed-phase partitioning, and planetary albedo in GCMs. *Journal of Advances in Modeling Earth Systems*. doi:10.1002/2015MS000589.

McCoy, K., Tuck, E., & McKenzie, M. (2014). Special issue on land-based education: Indigenous, postcolonial, and decolonizing perspectives on place and environmental education research, volume 18. *Environmental Education Research*, *20*(1), 1–23. doi: 10.1080/13504622.2013.877708.

McGregor, D. (2000). The state of traditional ecological knowledge research in Canada: A critique of current theory and practice. In R. Laliberte,, P. Settee, J. Waldram, R. Innes, B. Macdougall, L. McBain, & F. Barron (Eds.). *Expressions in Canadian native studies*. Saskatoon, SK: University of Saskatchewan Extension Press.

McGregor, D. (2012). Traditional knowledge: Considerations for protecting water in Ontario. *International Indigenous Policy Journal, 3*.

McKenzie, M., Hart, P., Bai, H., & Jickling, B. (2009). Introduction: Educational fields and cultural imaginaries. In M. McKenzie, P. Hart, H. Bai, & B. Jickling (Eds.), *Fields of green: Restorying culture, environment, and education* (pp. 1–11). Cresskill, NJ: Hampton.

Mead, G. H. (1934). *Mind, self and society*. Chicago: University of Chicago Press.

Mey, W. (Ed.) (1984). *Genocide in the Chittagong Hill tracts, Bangladesh*. Document No. 51. Copenhagen: International Workgroup for Indigenous Affairs (IWGIA).

Meyer, M. A. (2001). Acultural assumptions of empiricism: A native Hawaiian critique. *Canadian Journal of Native Education*, *25*(2), 188–200.

Meyer, M. A. (2008). Indigenous and authentic: Hawaiian epistemology and the triangulation of meaning. In N. K. Denzin, Y. S. Lincoln, & L. T. Smith (Eds.), *Handbook of critical and Indigenous methodologies* (pp. 211–216). Berkeley, CA: Sage.

Mitchell, W. J. T. (1995). Translator translated (interview with cultural theorist Homi Bhabha). *Artforum*, 80–84.

Mohsin, A. (1997). *The politics of nationalism: The case of the Chittagong Hill tracts*. Dhaka, Bangladesh: The University Press.

Mohsin, A. (2002). *The polities of nationalism: The case of the Chittagong Hill tracts, Bangladesh*. Dhaka, Bangladesh: The University Press.

Nadasdy, P. (1999). The politics of TEK: power and the "integration" of knowledge. *Arctic Anthropology*, *36*, 1–18.

Nadasdy, P. (2003). *Hunters and bureaucrats: Power, knowledge and Aboriginal-state relations in the southwest Yukon*. Vancouver: UBC Press.

Nadasdy, P. (2007). The gift in the animal: The ontology of hunting and human-animal sociality. *American Ethnologist*, *34*(1), 25–43.

Nadasdy, P. (2011). We don't harvest animals: We kill them: Agricultural metaphors and the politics of wildlife management in the Yukon. In M. Goldman, P. Nadasdy, & M. D. Turner (Eds.), *Knowing management* (pp. 135–151). Chicago: The University of Chicago Press.

Natcher, D. C., & Clifford, G. H. (2007). Putting the community back into community-based resource management. In D. C. Natcher (Ed.), *Seeing beyond the trees: The social dimensions of aboriginal forest management* (pp. 41–59). Concord, Ontario: Captus Press.

Nath, T. K., & Inoue, M. (2009). Forest based settlement project and its impact on community livelihood in Chittagong Hill tracts, Bangladesh. *International Forestry Review*, *11*, 394–407. doi: 10.1505/ifor.11.3.394.

Nelson, M. (2006). Paradigm shifts in aboriginal cultures?: Understanding TEK in historical and cultural context. *The Canadian Journal of Native Studies*, *XXV*(1), 289–310.

Parkin, R. (1997). Tree marriage in India. In S. Klaus (Ed.), *Management is culture: Indigenous knowledge and socio-cultural aspects of trees and forests in non-European culture* (pp. 51–57). London: Intermediate Technology Publication.

Patton, M. Q. (1990). *Qualitative evaluation and research methods*. Newbury Park, CA: Sage.

Patton, M. Q. (Ed.) (2002). *Qualitative research and evaluation methods*. Thousand Oaks, CA: Sage.

Payne, P. (2009). Postmodern oikos. In M. McKenzie, P. Hart, H. Bai, & B. Jickling (Eds.), *Fields of green: Restorying culture, environment, and education* (pp. 309–322). Cresskill, NJ: Hampton.

Pieterse, J. N. (2004). *Global and culture*. Lanham, ML: Rowman and Littlefield Publishers, Inc. Press.

Prothom Alo (2015, June 15). http://archive.prothom-alo.com/detail/news/131339

Roy, C. R. (2000). *Land rights of the Indigenous peoples of the Chittagong Hill tracts, Bangladesh*. Document No. 99. Copenhagen: International Workgroup for Indigenous Affairs (IWGIA).

Roy, R. D. (1996). Land rights: Land use and Indigenous Peoples in the Chittagong Hill Tracts. In P. Gain (Ed.), *Bangladesh: Land, forest and forest people* (pp. 53–118). Dhaka: Society for Environment and Human Development (SEHD).

Roy, R. D. (2002). *Land and forest rights in the Chittagong Hill tracts, Bangladesh*. ICIMOD Talking Points 4/02. Kathmandu: International Centre for Integrated Mountain Development. doi: 10.1080/14735903.2005.9684751.

Said, E. (1993). *Culture and imperialism*. London: Chatto & Windus.

Saldaña, J. (2010). *The coding manual for qualitative researchers*. London: Sage.

Schendel, V. W., Mey, W., & Dewan, K. A. (2001). *The Chittagong Hill tracts: Living in a borderland*. Dhaka, Bangladesh: The University Press.

Shiva, V. (2005). *Earth democracy: Justice, sustainability, and peace*. Cambridge, MA: South End Press.

Simpson, L. (2001). Aboriginal peoples and knowledge: Decolonizing our processes. *Canadian Journal of Native Studies*, *21*(1), 137–148.

Simpson, L. (2014). *Dancing on our turtle's back: Stories of Nishnaabeg re-creation, resurgence and a new emergence*. Winnipeg: ARP Books.

Smith, L. T. (1999). *Decolonizing methodologies: Research and indigenous peoples*. London: Zed Books.

Smith, L. T. (2006). Choosing the margins: The role of research in indigenous struggles for social justice. In N. K. Denzin & M. D. Giardina (Eds.), *Qualitative inquiry and the conservative challenge* (pp. 151–174). Walnut Creek, CA: Left Coast Press.

Smith, L. T. (2008). Choosing the margins: The role of research in indigenous struggles for social justice. In N. K. Denzin & M. D. Giardina (Eds.), *Qualitative inquiry and the conservative challenge* (pp. 151–174). Walnut Creek, CA: Left Coast Press.

Spivak, G. C. (2006). *Can the subaltern speak?* In B. Ashcroft, G. Griffiths, & H. Tiffin (Eds.), *The neo-colonial studies reader* (pp. 28–37). New York, NY: Routledge.

Stoecker, Randy. (2013). *Research methods for community change: A project-based approach*. Thousand Oaks, CA: Sage.

Stuckey, P. (2010). Being known by a birch tree: Animist refigurings of Western epistemology. *Journal for the Study of Religion, Nature & Culture*, *4*(3), 182–205.

Sumara, D. J. (1996). Using commonplace books in curriculum studies. *JCT Journal of Curriculum Theorizing*, *12*, 45–48.

Tanner, T. (1980). Significant life experiences. *The Journal of Environmental Education*, *11*(4), 20–24.

References

Thapa, G. B., & Rasul, G. (2006). Implications of changing national policies on land use in the Chittagong Hill tracts of Bangladesh. *Journal of Environmental Management, 81,* 441–453. doi: 10.1016/j.jenvman.2005.12.002.

Thompson, S. (2013), 'Taone Tupu Ora: Indigenous knowledge and sustainable Urban design', *GEOGRAPHICAL RESEARCH, 51,* 329–330, http://dx.doi.org/10.1111/j.1745-5871.2012.00783.x

Thrupp, L. A. (1998). Legitimizing local knowledge: From displacement to empowerment for third world people. *Agriculture and Human Values: Summer Issue,* 13–24.

Torre, M. E., & Ayala, J. (2009). Envisioning participatory action research entremundos. *Feminism and Psychology, 19*(3), 387–393.

Tuck, E. (2009). Re-visioning action: Participatory action research and Indigenous theories of change. *Urban Review, 41,* 47–65.

Tuck, E. & McKenzie, M. (2015). *Place in research: Theory, methodology, methods.* New York, NY: Routledge.

Tuck, E., & McKenzie, M. (2016). *Place in research: Theories, methodologies, methods.* New York: Routledge.

Tuck, E., McKenzie, M., & McCoy, K. (2014). Land education: Indigenous, post-colonial, and decolonizing perspectives on place and environmental education research. *Environmental Education Research, 20,* 1–23.

Tuck, E., & Yang, K. W. (2012). Decolonization is not a metaphor. *Decolonization: Indigeneity, Education and Society, 1,* 1–40.

United Nations Declaration (2008). *Guidelines on Indigenous Peoples' issues,* United Nations Development Group, 1. http://www.converge.org.nz/pma/dec1108.htm

United Nations Development Programme. (2013, December). *Bangladesh report.* Retrieved from http://hdr.undp.org/en/2013-report.

Vos, R. O. (2007). Defining sustainability: A conceptual orientation. *Journal of Chemical Technology and Biotechnology, 82,* 334–339.

Wainwright, J., & Barnes, T. (2009). Management, economy, and the space – Place distinction. *Environment and Planning D: Society and Space, 27*(6), 966–986.

Walker, K., & Le, M. (2008), Neoliberalism on the ground in rural India: Predatory growth, agrarian crisis, internal colonization, and the intensification of class struggle. *Journal of Peasant Studies, 35*(4), 557–620.

Walker, R, Ted, J., & David, C. N. (Eds.), (2013). *Reclaiming Indigenous planning.* Montreal: McGill-Queen's University Press.

Wallerstein, N. B., & Duran, B. (2006). Using community-based participatory research to address health disparities. *Health Promotion Practice, 7*(3), 312–323.

Watson, A. (2013). Misunderstanding the 'nature' of co-management: A geography of regulatory science and Indigenous knowledges (IK). *Environmental Management,* 52(5), (2013), 1085–1102, 10.1007/s00267-013-0111-z

Whatmore, S. (2002). *Hybrid geographies: Managements, cultures, spaces.* London: Routledge.

Whatmore, S. (2006). Materialist returns: Practising cultural geography in and for a more-than-human world. *Cultural Geographies, 13.* doi: 10.1191/1474474006cgj377oa.

Wilson, A., & Pence, E. (2010). U.S. Legal interventions the lives of battered women: An Indigenous assessment. *Justice as Healing: A Newsletter on Aboriginal Concepts of Justice, 15*(1), 1–6.

Wilson, S. (2007). Guest editorial: What is an indigenist research paradigm? *Canadian Journal of Native Education, 30*(2), 193–195, University of Alberta, Faculty of

Education. Retrieved from http://search.proquest.com/docview/230305972?accountid=14771.

Wilson, S. (2008). *Research is ceremony: Indigenous research methods*. Winnipeg, Manitoba: Fernwood Publisher.

Wilson, S. (2013). Using indigenist research to shape our future. In M. Gray, J. Coates, M. Yellow Bird, & T. Hetherington (Eds.), *Decolonizing social work*. Burlington, VT: Ashgate.

Young, R. (2003), *Postcolonialism: A very short introduction*. New York: Oxford University Press.

Index

actor 13, 19, 23–34, 49–50, 56, 59, 66, 77, 104, 131–2, 133
actor network theory 24, 49, 59
advocacy 38, 107, 122
agriculture domain 63, 65–6, 70
ancestor stories 105–6
anti-community development projects 2, 14, 52, 86, 101–2, 110–11, 126

Bandarban district 9, 12, 16–18, 111
Bangladesh Forest Department Policy (BFDP) 90
Bangladesh Forest Industries Development Corporation (BFIDC) 92, 94, 100
Bangladeshi administrative power 87, 90
Bangladeshi Administrative Structure 87
Bangladeshi governance 87
belongingness 16, 55, 57
Bhabha, Homi 23–6, 60, 114, 133
Binni crop 66
Bloch, Maurice 28
Bogle puja 58, 75
building trustful relationships 35, 48–9

call to implications 20, 125–30
cattle 58, 67, 69, 79, 89, 90
ceremony/ceremonies X, 6, 9, 53, 73, 76, 78
challenges 3, 6–7, 13, 21–2, 27, 36, 47–50, 64, 113, 24–7, 29–32, 61, 74, 82, 126
Circle Chiefs 70–1, 73–4
colonial/colonialism 7, 10–14, 20, 74, 84, 87, 101–2, 112, 134
Commonplace Books 17, 42, 44–6, 48, 52, 55
community meanings of management 26, 29, 31, 64–70, 79–82

community's perceptions of current management 84–102
community's perceptions of environmental sustainability 104–17
community's perceptions of land-water 55–9
community-based research ethics 47
community-based sustainability 105, 114
co-researcher participants 11, 18, 19, 35–6, 40–53
cross-cultural identity 37, 39
cultivation and production spirituality 75
cultivation tools 51, 56, 63, 65, 68–70, 80
customary practices 73, 111, 117, 120

danger 25, 86, 93–6, 101, 110–11
data analysis 11, 41–6, 51–4, 84, 105
data collection stories 17, 40, 42, 44
decision-making processes 12, 37, 77, 88, 109–12
decolonization ix–x, 9–10
deforestation 47, 91, 94–5, 101–2
Deleuze, Gilles 23–4, 26
development projects 1–3, 8–10, 14, 17, 52, 86, 101–2, 109–11, 123, 126, 128–9
diverse knowledge x, 81
domestic animals 51, 58, 65, 69, 76, 80–1, 90, 95
dreams 33, 52, 105, 107–8

economic domains 78–9, 83
educational Curriculum 119, 122
Elders and Knowledge-holders 10, 11, 44, 46, 48–9, 51–2, 55–8, 63
Elders, Knowledge-holders, and leaders 41, 79, 94, 101, 109–10, 117
eliminate poverty 109
empowering Participants 35, 49

environmental sustainability x, 1–2, 4, 7–9, 38, 58, 104, 105–24
Escobar, Arturo 23–5, 29, 31–3, 102, 114
ethnic diversity 16–7
exploitation 5, 7, 13, 85–6, 94, 102, 114, 121

fear 6, 85–6, 98
forest resources 65–7, 70, 72–3, 83, 88, 92, 96, 98, 11, 110–11
forms of neocolonialism 100
foundation of hybridity 60
frustration 85–6
future research 127, 129–30

gifts 45, 67–9, 113
global positioning system (GPS) 103
God 25, 28, 31, 56–8, 62, 63, 69, 75–7, 106, 131

hanei puja 75–6
headman 70–4
hilly land 10, 67, 75, 78–9, 100
holism 51–3
holistic 1, 3, 28, 32, 36, 49, 50, 80, 115, 123
honor 2–4, 8, 10–11, 19, 29, 35–6, 49, 50 53, 56, 58–9, 62, 68, 71, 75–7, 81, 106, 106, 120
hopes 4–5, 14, 20, 52, 104–5, 107–8, 115, 123
hybrid practices 59, 114
hybridity 122–5, 59–61, 114

identity 30, 36–9, 57, 60–1, 74, 78, 102, 104, 105, 109, 117, 120, 122, 125
illegal logging 92–5, 101
indigenous voices 61, 51
individual story sharing 17, 43–5, 55, 84, 110
Ingold, Tim 23, 26, 28, 32
interconnectedness 55–6, 59
interviews 42, 44, 48, 52
invisible displacement 97–8
invisible negative impacts 97

Jhum crop 66
journey of ceremony 6–7

Kantu Khyeng 10, 18
Karbary 47, 71–4, 83, 95
knife 68–9
knowledge ownership 49

land spirituality 65, 78, 64–82
Latour, Bruno 22–6, 32, 61, 81, 124
learning traditional cultivation systems 117–18
Levi-Strauss 23–6, 133
local knowledge and practice 64
lokki puja 76
lumber plantations 86, 91–3, 110, 128, 134
lung puja 75–6

mainstream community 7, 37, 41, 69, 74, 109–10, 117, 122
management as agency 37, 81
medicine people 81
methodology 17, 26, 35–6, 39, 42, 44–5, 49, 53–4, 133
methods 1, 9, 10, 17, 26, 29, 36, 42–3, 49, 53, 55, 64, 64, 93, 120
minority 12, 18, 37–9, 41, 54, 126
Moussa 70, 71, 74, 87

neocolonial 10, 13–4, 18, 21, 26, 29, 30, 100
networking 121
NGOs 6, 8, 20, 30, 49, 73, 84, 107, 113, 123, 127

orientalism 105
otherness 22–3, 25–6, 36, 102, 133

participant guidelines 52
participant observation 11, 17, 38, 41–2, 45, 54–5, 96, 106
participants' perspectives 5, 10, 88
participants' selection 41
participatory action research 2–3, 10, 17, 19, 27, 35–8, 42, 48, 51, 53–5
participatory data collection stories 42
participatory methodology 45
peace accord 110, 127, 130
peaceful demonstrations 126
personal reflections 18, 41, 43–4, 127, 130
photovoice 11, 17, 42–6, 53, 54, 61, 82, 84
pig 67, 69, 79, 90
plain land 45, 51, 66–70, 71, 76–9, 82–5, 89, 91, 94, 96, 100, 106–11, 118, 127
plain-land crops 66–7
poem 11, 41, 44, 59, 66, 74
policy and practice 20, 127
poverty 85–6, 90, 94–7, 100–2, 109–13
power disparity 87
practice-based 33, 80, 114

148 Index

practicing spirituality 120
preservation and promotion 119
private brickfield project 88–92, 97
promotion of community music, dance, and stories 119
protect traditional customary practices 120
puja 75–8

raja/king 47, 70–3
readers 8–9
reclaim and reconnect 125
relational accountabilities 50–1
relational ontology 2, 17, 19, 22–36, 50, 133
relational practice 17, 20, 22, 27–8, 32, 51, 62–3, 80, 106, 114
relationality 17, 20, 22, 27–8, 32, 51, 62–3, 80, 106, 107, 115, 133
research and activism 126
research as exploitation 5
research site 17, 19, 35, 39–42, 48, 52, 72
reserve forest 92, 100, 111
respect 4, 8, 11, 14, 16, 26, 28, 30, 33, 36, 38, 39, 42, 48, 49, 50–8, 62, 65–7, 105–6, 114, 116, 120, 124, 130
responsibilities 3, 6, 19–20, 36–41, 48–53, 56, 56, 59, 70–4, 104–30

sacred places 58–9
safety 48
Said, Edward 25–6, 63, 102, 133
settler bengali workers 89
smells 23, 55, 105, 107–9, 115
socialization 36–7, 39
song 110, 117, 119
soyttobill puja 75, 77
spear 68, 69
species diversity 82, 93, 97, 100, 109
species loss 100
spiritual and emotional connection 131
spiritual and relational management 61, 82, 131
spiritual practice and management 74
spiritual role in sustainability management 108

spirituality 1–3, 14, 19, 22–3, 27, 28, 31, 42, 51, 53, 55–7, 62, 65, 67, 72, 74–7, 104–10, 115, 117, 120–2, 129–30
stone spirituality 75
subaltern 30
subsistence crops 67
sword 68–9

theoretical framework 1, 17, 22–36, 131–4, 51, 55–6, 83, 124
things 19, 22–4, 33
third space 22
tobacco plantation 20, 45, 47, 52, 84, 86, 94–8, 103, 112, 122
tobacco plantation and management 94
traditional administrative structure 13, 64, 70–1, 80, 83, 87–8
traditional cultivation culture 16, 62–3, 70, 105–6, 109, 111, 115–17, 127–9, 133–4
traditional economy 55, 65, 78
traditional land-water management 2, 13, 19, 64
traditional modes of administrative structure 55–7
traditional sharing circles 11, 17, 41–3, 54
traditional weaving 120–1
travel advisory 39–41
types of paddy 65–6, 80–1

violent political situation 48

water spirituality 57, 75
Western management 2, 6, 29–31, 86, 125
Western research 19, 27, 35, 38, 53, 133
Western science 19, 63–4, 117
Whatmore, Sarah 2–26, 33, 61, 114
Wilson, Shawn ix–xi, 5–6, 8, 17, 22, 27, 36–7, 53, 133
women's disempowerment 97

youth responsibilities 116–23